Advances in Communications, Computing, Networks and Security Volume 11

Proceedings of the MSc/MRes Programmes from the School of Computing and Mathematics

2012 - 2013

Editor

Dr Paul S Dowland

School of Computing and Mathematics
Plymouth University

ISBN: 978-1-84102-374-8

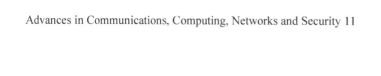

Preface

This book is the ninth in a series presenting research papers arising from MSc/MRes research projects undertaken by students of the School of Computing and Mathematics at Plymouth University. These one year masters courses include a significant period of full-time project activity, and students are assessed on the basis of an MSc or MRes thesis, plus an accompanying research paper.

The publications in this volume are based upon research projects that were undertaken during the 2012/13 academic year. A total of 15 papers are presented, covering many aspects of modern networking and communication technology, including security, mobility, coding schemes and quality measurement. Specifically contributing programmes are: Communication Engineering and Signal Processing, Computer and Information Security, Network Systems Engineering, Robotics, and Web Technologies and Security.

The authorship of the papers is credited to the MSc/MRes student in each case (appearing as the first named author), with other authors being the academic supervisors that had significant input into the projects. Indeed, the projects were conducted in collaboration with supervisors from the internationally recognised research groups within the School, and the underlying research projects are typically related to wider research initiatives with which these groups are involved. Readers interested in further details of the related research areas are therefore encouraged to make contact with the academic supervisors, using the contact details provided elsewhere in this publication.

Each of the papers presented here is also supported by a full MSc or MRes thesis, which contains more comprehensive details of the work undertaken and the results obtained. Copies of these documents are also in the public domain, and can generally be obtained upon request via inter-library loan.

We believe that these papers have value to the academic community, and we therefore hope that their publication in this volume will be of interest to you.

Dr Paul Dowland

School of Computing and Mathematics
Plymouth University, August 2014

About the School of Computing and Mathematics

The School of Computing and Mathematics has interests spanning the interface between computing and electronics, through software, networks, and communications. The School contains 61 academic staff and has over 1500 students enrolled on its portfolio of taught courses, over 50 of which are at MSc level. In addition there are over 100 postgraduate research students enrolled on a variety of research programmes, most of which enjoy sponsorship from external sources.

This School sits alongside four other Schools in the Faculty of Science and Environment, the School of Biological Sciences, the School of Geography, Earth and Environmental Sciences, and, the School of Marine Science and Engineering. There are research and teaching links across all four schools as well as with the rest of the University.

Prof. Steven Furnell
Head of School

Contributing Research Centres

Centre for Robotics and Neural Systems

Head: Professor Angelo Cangelosi
Email: angelo.cangelosi@plymouth.ac.uk
Research interests:
1) Cognitive systems
2) Social interaction and concept formation through human-robot interaction
3) Artificial intelligence techniques and human-robot interfaces
4) Cooperative mobile robots
5) Visual perception of natural objects
6) Humanoid robots

https://www1.plymouth.ac.uk/research/crns/

Centre for Security, Communications and Network Research

Head: Professor S M Furnell
E-mail info@cscan.org
Research interests:
1) Information systems security
2) Internet and Web technologies and applications
3) Mobile applications and services
4) Network management

http://www.cscan.org

Signal Processing and Multimedia Communications

Head: Professor E Ifeachor BSc, MSc, PhD, DIC, CEng, MIEE
E-mail e.ifeachor@plymouth.ac.uk
Research interests:
1) Multimedia communications
2) Audio and bio-signal processing
3) Bioinformatics

http://www.tech.plymouth.ac.uk/spmc/

Contents

Evaluation of Power Consumption in Mobile
A Case Study of Multimedia Applications

S.Alalaji and L.Sun

Center for Security, Communications and Network Research,
Plymouth University, Plymouth, United Kingdom
e-mail: info@cscan.org

Abstract

Smartphone technology has, until recently, been developing rapidly, and is still continuing to evolve. There has been significant development in components such as processors, memory and multimedia applications. However multimedia applications in smartphones use a considerable amount of power compared to other components. Consequently, power conservation has become an important issue for researchers around the world. Some research have been investigated the impact of network media such as 2G, 3G and WiFi on the total power of mobile phone.

This project concentrates on investigating the power consumption of a multimedia application (IMSDroid) on different Android mobile phones (Samsung Galaxy S3, Samsung Galaxy ACE and HTC Magic) using different video movements (Akiyo, Foreman and Stefan). The videos were converted to H.264 video codec with different send bitrates and then sent to IMSDroid using two multimedia applications (Boghe IMS Client and Linphone). In addition, the quality of mobile videos on Boghe IMS Client has been evaluated on different Android mobile phones with 512Kbps bitrate and different resolusions.

The results show that when Boghe IMS Client was used, the power consumption of IMSDroid for Akiyo, Foreman and Stefan 512Kbps decreased with the increase of mobile firmware and resolusions in different mobile phones. Furthermore, the power consumption increases with the increase of bitrates when send fast movements on Linphone application. In addition, the quality evaluation for Akiyo, Foreman and Stefan increased with the increase of resolusions in different mobile phones.

Keywords

Power, IMSDroid, Boghe IMS Client, SIP, H264, WLAN, Android, Quality.

1   Introduction

Mobile device technology has developed significantly over recent years, e.g. the CPU and the memory. However, the battery has not kept up with these developments. At the same time, multimedia applications (such as YouTube and Skype) are used significantly in mobile devices, leading to the consumption of a considerable amount of power. Therefore, the growth of power consumption in games and multimedia has increased the concerns relating to energy conservation. In addition, there has been increased motivation amongst researchers to develop a technique to save energy in mobile phones. A number of studies have been conducted in order to reduce the power consumption of multimedia applications. Some researchers have tended to concentrate on evaluating the power consumption of voice and video codecs during multimedia communication.

This paper investigates the power consumption of a multimedia application on different Android mobile phones using different video movements. In addition, evaluates the quality of mobile videos on different mobile phones under different resolusions in order to see whether they have an impact on video quality.

2   Related work

Power consumption in mobile phones has been investigated from different angles. Some concentrate on network related factors, such as signal quality and network load. Others investigate power consumption in terms of network media (2G, 3G and WiFi) while others demonstrate the effect of changing the codecs and sending bitrates (SBR) on the power and the percentage that might be saved when using these methods.

Rice and Hay (2010) propose a framework that analyses the power consumption in two android mobile phones in terms of 2G and 3G. The results show that the idle power consumed when connected to 2G is higher than 3G or WiFi.. Csernai and Gulyás, (2011) claim that up to 30% of the total power consumption can be saved when using QoE estimation algorithm that estimates the video quality and then controls the sleep cycles of the wireless network adapter depending on the QoE. Mkwawa and Sun (2012) investigated the power consumption on mobile phones in terms of changing the voice and video sending bitrates to reduce the power consumption while keeping the quality at an acceptable level. They argued that the total power consumed in the Android phone can be saved by 10 – 30 % when using this scheme.

In this paper, the power consumption for a multimedia application will be investigated on different Android mobile phones to establish the impact of different mobile phones on the power consumption. Moreover, the video quality will be evaluated on the same mobile phones to see whether different resolusions have an impact on the video quality.

3   Testbed Setup and Results

The testbed consists of several components that help to carry out a video call from Boghe IMS Client (Doubango, 2012) and Linphone (Linphone, 2013) to IMSDroid (Doubango, 2012), in order to calculate the power consumption for IMSDroid on different mobile phones (Figure 1). The testbed consists of two client machines and one server, which are connected to each other through a wireless network: the first client is a laptop that consists of FFmpeg tool (FFmpeg, 2013) that used to convert video format to H264 video format and ManyCam tool (ManyCam, 2013) to inject the video to the sender. The second client consists of an Android mobile phone that has IMSDroid and the PowerTutor (Umich, 2011) tool to monitor power. The server is another laptop, which has Asterisk Server running on the Ubuntu Linux system to pass the video call between clients. To carry out the video call, three different video movements were used (Akiyo, Foreman and Stefan) with different sending bitrate. These videos were injected to the sender using ManyCam and then the power consumption of IMSDroid was measured using PowerTutor.

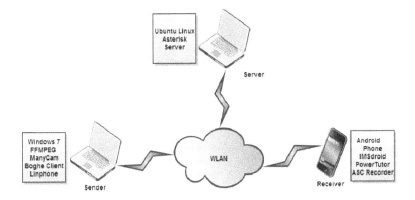

Figure 1: Testbed architecture

4 Results

This section will demonstrate the main results of the power consumption for IMSDroid on Samsung Galaxy S3, Samsung Galaxy ACE and HTC Magic mobile phones when Boghe and Linphone softphone were used and whether different mobile phones have an impact on the power consumption. In addition, the video quality evaluation for the mobile phones with different resolusions will be illustrated.

4.1 Power consumption of IMSDroid on Boghe IMS Client

The power consumption of IMSDroid under Boghe IMS Client was investigated on different Android mobile phones using different video movements (Akiyo, Foreman and Stefan) using 512Kbps bitrate. All results will be shown in this section.

4.1.1 Akiyo

It is clear from Figure 2 that the power consumption for Akiyo in Galaxy S3 that has high resolusions is lower than Galaxy ACE and HTC Magic. In addition, the power consumed to decode the same video in Galaxy ACE is higher than HTC Magic even though the resolusions are the same.

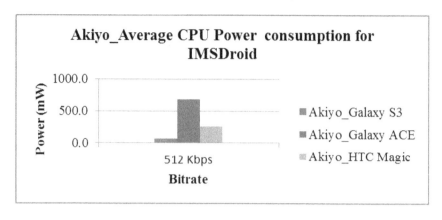

Figure 2: Power consumption for Akiyo

4.1.2 Foreman

The power consumption for Foreman 512Kbps in the three mobile phones was plotted in Figure 3.

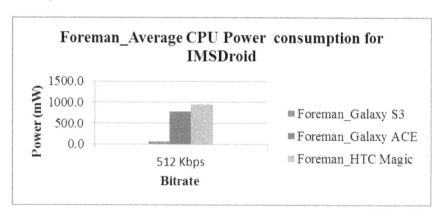

Figure 3: Power consumption for Foreman

The results show that the power consumption for Foreman in HTC Magic that has low resolusions is the highest followed by Galaxy ACE. However, Galaxy S3 decoded the same video using less than 100mW. In general, the power consumption for IMSDroid decreased with the increase of resolusions and mobile firmware.

4.1.3 Stefan

Figure 4 illustrates the power consumption for Stefan 512Kbps in the three mobile phones.

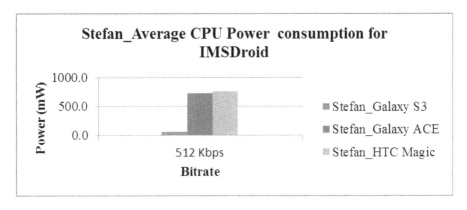

Figure 4: Power consumption for Stefan

The results show the power consumption for Stefan in HTC is slightly higher than Galaxy ACE. Moreover, there is a big difference in the power consumption in Galaxy ACE and HTC Magic when compared with Galaxy S3 which decoded the same video using less than 100mW. In general, the power consumption for IMSDroid decreased with the increase of resolusions and mobile firmware.

To sum up, the power consumption for Akiyo, Foreman and Stefan 512Kbps decreased with the increase of mobile firmware and resolusions in different mobile phones. However, the power consumption for Akiyo 512Kbps in Galaxy ACE which has the same resolusions with HTC Magic was increased.

4.2   Power consumption of IMSDroid on Linphone

The power consumption of IMSDroid on Linphone was investigated using two methods: different video movements with different bitrates and one video with different bitrates in order to find out whether or not different bitrates have an impact on the power consumption. All experiments will be carried out on Samsung Galaxy ACE mobile phone.

4.2.1   CPU of IMSDroid when using different videos with different bitrates

The power consumption for IMSDroid was investigated using Foreman and Stefan video movements and the following bitrates: 512Kbps, 1Mbps and 2Mbps. Figure 5 displays the results.

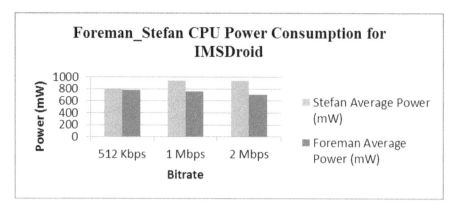

Figure 5: Power consumption for Foreman and Stefan

The power consumption for IMSDroid decreased with the increase of sending bitrate for Foreman video movement. However, the power increases with the increase of bitrate for Stefan videos.

4.2.2 CPU of IMSDroid when using one video with different bitrates

In this section, Stefan 2Mbps movement was used with different bitrates in order to investigate the power of IMSDroid to find out the correlation between the power consumption and different bitrates. In addition, the results will be compared with the power consumption when using different videos with different bitrate.

Figure 6 demonstrates the power consumption for IMSDroid with different bitrates for Stefan 2Mbps.

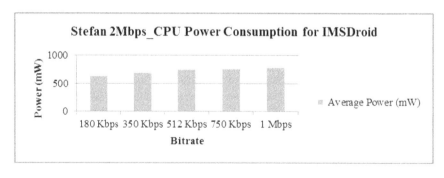

Figure 6: Power consumption for Stefan 2Mbps

It is clear from figure 6 that all power values for IMSDroid are increased with the increase of sending bitrate which is the same results when using different videos of Stefan with different send bitrates.

To sum up, only Stefan (fast movement) that proves the power consumption increases with the increase of bitrate on Linphone.

4.3   Quality evaluation for different mobile phones

The video quality evaluation for Akiyo, Foreman and Stefan using 512Kbps bitrate on Galaxy S3, Galaxy ACE and HTC Magic will be illustrated in this section in order to establish whether different resolusions have an impact on the video quality. Quality evaluation for Akiyo, Foreman and Stefan 2Mbps are demonstrated in Figures 7, 8 and 9.

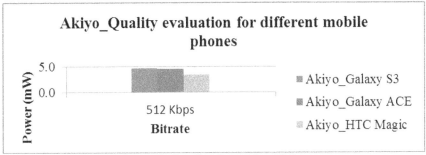

Figure 7: Quality for Akiyo 2Mbps

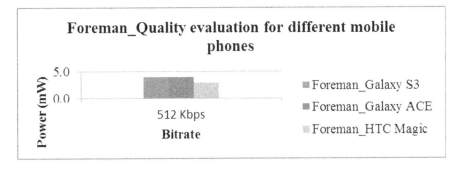

Figure 8: Quality for Foreman 2Mbps

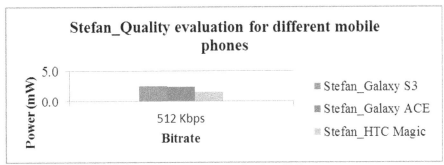

Figure 9: Quality for Stefan 2Mbps

It is clear from Figures 7, 8 and 9 that the quality evaluation for Akiyo, Foreman and Stefan 512Kbps respectively increased with the increase of resolusions in different mobile phones.

5 Conclusion and future work

This paper investigates the power consumption of IMSDroid on different Android mobile phone using Boghe IMS Client and Linphone. The results show only Stefan (fast movement) that proves the power consumption increases with the increase of bitrate on Linphone while Akiyo, Foreman and Stefan 512Kbps decreased with the increase of mobile firmware and resolusions on Boghe IMS Client.

The future work can include other different video codecs with other different bitrate. In addition, it might include other multimedia application that can work properly under WiFi or high speed data mobile phone such as 4G. Furthermore, using techniques to send bitrate intelligently using programming could be involved. The future work can also include quality evaluation with network parameter such as delay and packet loss to establish the impact on the power consumption and quality under different mobile phones.

6 References

Csernai, M., & Gulyás, A. (2011) 'Wireless adapter sleep scheduling based on video QoE: How to improve battery life when watching streaming video?'. In *Computer Communications and Networks (ICCCN), 2011 Proceedings of 20th International Conference on.* Maui, Hawaii. 31 July - 4 August 201. IEEE.

Doubango (2012) *boghe - IMS/RCS client for Windows Phone 8, Surface and Desktop - Google Project Hosting.* Available at: https://code.google.com/p/boghe (Accessed: 21 June 2013).

Doubango (2012) *imsdroid - High Quality Video SIP/IMS client for Google Android - Google Project Hosting.* Available at: https://code.google.com/p/imsdroid/ (Accessed: 21 June 2013).

FFmpeg (2013) ffmpeg. Available at: http://www.ffmpeg.org/ (Accessed: 22 June 2013).

Linphone (2013) *About Linphone | Linphone, an open-source video sip phone.* Available at: http://www.linphone.org/eng/linphone/about.html (Accessed: 10 August 2013).

ManyCam (2013) ManyCam free virtual webcam effects software. Available at: http://www.manycam.com/ (Accessed: 22 June 2013).

Mkwawa, I. H., & Sun, L. (2012) 'Power-driven VoIP quality adaptation over WLAN in mobile devices'. In Globecom Workshops (GC Wkshps), 2012 IEEE (pp. 1276-1281). IEEE. .[Online].Available at: http://ieeexplore.ieee.org/stamp/stamp.jsp?tp=&arnumber=6477765 (Accessed: 29 December 2012).

Rice, A., & Hay, S. (2010) 'Decomposing power measurements for mobile devices'. In *Pervasive Computing and Communications (PerCom.) 2010 IEEE International Conference on.* Mannheim, Germany. 29 March −2 April, 2010.IEEE. Available at: http://www.cl.cam.ac.uk/~acr31/pubs/rice-power.pdf (Accessed: 7 January 2013).

Umich (2011) *A Power Monitor for Android-Based Mobile Platforms.* Available at: http://ziyang.eecs.umich.edu/projects/powertutor/ (Accessed: 16 June 2013).

Performance Analysis for Skype Video Call based on Mobile Devices over WLAN

A.Alfaifi and L.Sun

Center for Security, Communications and Network Research,
Plymouth University, Plymouth, United Kingdom
e-mail: info@cscan.org

Abstract

Most Internet users today prefer to use VoIP (Voice over Internet Protocol) for voice and video communications over the Internet because of its powerful features, including flexibility, cost savings, and the high quality of services when compared to traditional communication or public switched telephone networks (PSTN). Skype is the most popular VoIP technology. It provides users with the best quality for voice and video calls under different network conditions. In addition, it is available over mobile devices, which gives users the advantage of making video calls through their smartphones. Many researchers have conducted studies on the nature of Skype over the Internet in order to explore its adaptation techniques and features. However, limited work has been carried out on Skype performance in mobile environment. This paper concentrates on investigating the performance of Skype's video quality in terms of sending rate, packet size, and inter-packet gap when using mobile devices under different signal strengths over Wireless LAN. Furthermore, the end user's quality of experience (QoE) in terms of Mean Opinion Score (MOS) is assessed via informal subjective tests and user acceptance of quality under different RSSI was investigated. The preliminary results show that Skype can adapt efficiently to signal strength (expressed by Received Signal Strength Indicator, RSSI) variations. We have also observed that most users accept Skype's quality when RSSI reaches -85 dBm or more, but they will not tolerate the quality when the RSSI decreases below that level.

Keywords

Skype, video call, RSSI, QoE.

1 Introduction

The Internet today has increased in popularity exponentially and has led to an evolution of several communication technologies. When the Internet first became prominent, email and text messages were the first means of communication. However, recently the most efficient way of communication is voice and video over IP (VoIP). Many video applications have been produced by different companies such as MSN Messenger, X-Lite, and Google Talk. Skype, however, is the most popular VoIP application. It provides users with the best quality of voice and video calls under different network conditions. Recent statistics illustrate the massive number of users subscribed to Skype's service in order to establish video calls or video conferencing over the Internet using fixed computers or mobile devices such as PDAs and smartphones. Due to the increased use of smartphones and PDAs, Skype offers several free versions that work on different smartphone platforms. This gives users the opportunity to make video calls using smartphones while they move about in different places, such as airports, malls, universities, etc. As such, the signal strength between the smartphone/PDA and access points plays an important role in Skype's performance and quality. It is therefore very important for developers, researchers, and users to evaluate the performance of Skype's video calls under different signal strength conditions.

In this paper, we endeavour to investigate Skype's video call performance under different signal strength levels using mobile devices over Wireless LAN. In addition, the quality of experience (QoE) of users was measured and user quality acceptance under different RSSI values was investigated via subjective tests.

2   Related work

Several studies have been conducted on Skype's video call performance under several network conditions. Boyaci et al. (2009) and De Cicco et al. (2011) have studied the performance of Skype when applying different bandwidth rates. In their studies, they focused mostly on the Skype's sending rate and how bandwidth variation could affect it. They found that Skype adapts its sending bit rate appropriately when bandwidth rate changes. This mechanism helps Skype to avoid packet loss which will affect the video quality. Moreover, De Cicco et al. (2011) noticed that when bandwidth increased, Skype increased its sending rate and it decreased its rate when bandwidth decreased. On the other hand, Xinggong et al. (2012) have investigated the impact of packet loss on the Skype sending rate. They observed that when the packet loss rate is less than 10%, Skype reduces its video rate. This reduction allowed Skype to utilise the forward error correction algorithm (FEC) in order to resist this loss. When the packet loss rate increases to more than 10%, Skype decreases its sending rates and video rates. This will help the FEC mechanism to get adequate bandwidth to counter this loss. Moreover, Zhu (2011) studied the relationship between user experience (MOS) of Skype's video call and its sending rate. They observed that the minimum RSSI required to achieve good, fair and low quality based on MOS scores were -77, -82 and -85 respectively. In addition, Skype adjusted its sending rate from 5 kbps up to 60 Kbps while MOS score increased. Consequently, Mkwawa et al. (2012) also studied the relationship between the user experience of a Skype video call (i.e., QoE) and RSSI over a Wi-Fi network using mobile phones. They found that Zhu (2011) did not map RSSI to QoE in his experiment and he used RSSI for managing the handover purpose between 3G and WLAN. They discovered that an MOS score with an average of 4.2, provided excellent quality with RSSI values > -74 dBm. Also, when the RSSI values were between -74 and -80 dBm, MOS score was about 3.5 on average with good video quality, if RSSI was less than -80 dBm, the MOS value was about 2.5 with poor video quality. They also concluded that with low values of RSSI, there was a high rate of packet loss. They observed the packet losses occurred only when the RSSI value was < -75 dBm. In our paper, we will examine Skype performance under different RSSI values using different video motions. Finally, end users' experiences with Skype video quality will be measured.

3   Testbed Setup

A configured testbed that has different components was used to investigate Skype's video call performance over a mobile phone. Figure 1 shows the test bed which consists of one laptop (laptop2) and one smartphone (iPhone 4s with Apple iOS platform) on which the Skype software was installed. The smartphone is connected to laptop1 using Wi-Fi connection, while this laptop is connected to NAT wireless router which is connected to a 30 MB fibre optic cable provided by Virgin Media Company at residential area. Each host has a private IP address and connects to the Internet using this router. Two main tools were used on the smartphone: WiFiFoFum, which reads RSSI values from the router (WiFiFoFum, 2013), and Display Recorder to record videos during Skype's video calls. In order to emulate Skype's video calls, three standard video sequences with different speeds were used; Akiyo, Foreman and Coastguard were used in order to examine Skype's behaviour in different video motions (Figure 2). These videos are injected into Skype using ManyCam (ManyCam, 2013). Wireshark was used to capture data, which were then analysed using Matlab.

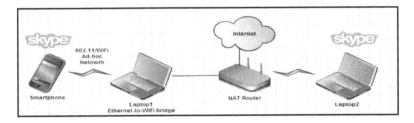

Figure 1: Testbed architecture

Figure 2: Snapshot of three different video sequences

4   Measurement Results

We will demonstrate in this section Skype's video call performance under different RSSI values. This includes reporting on the performance of Skype's video calls over a mobile phone in terms of sending rate and packet size; evaluating user's quality of experience (QoE); mapping RSSI values to average mean opinion scores (MOS) and deriving the relationship between RSSI and average MOS using the curve fitting technique for all video sequences at different motion speeds.

4.1   Impact of RSSI values on Skype's video call

We investigated how Skype behaves in terms of sending rate and packet size. RSSI values were changed according to the following selected values: -60,-70,-80,-85.-88,-90,-91 and -92 dBm using the WiFiFoFum tool over a smartphone device. These experiments were conducted for around five days and it took about six hours each day especially during the morning time to capture, evaluate and analyse the output in order to obtain the following findings.

The measurement findings of Skype's sending rate are demonstrated in Figure 3. We observed that Skype adapts its sending rates to different RSSI values in three stages. In the first stage with an RSSI value between -60 and -70 dBm, Skype's sending rate remained almost constant. In the second stage, when the RSSI was between -70 and -88 dBm, the sending rate decreased gradually. When the RSSI was less than -88 dBm, we observed a dramatic decrease in Skype's sending rate for all video sequences: that is, for slow, medium, and fast motion videos.

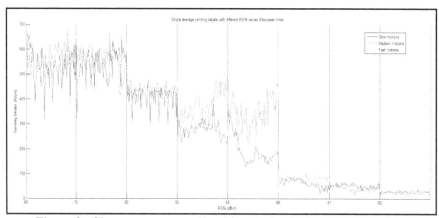

Figure 3: Skype average sending bit rate for different RSSI values

In summary, Skype's sending bit rate fluctuates every second in all videos as it attempts to adapt to the change of the signal strength between the smartphone and the router. As mentioned previously, there was a gradual decrease in the sending rates between -70 and -88 dBm after which the rate decreased dramatically, beginning at -88 dBm. This adaption in the sending rate was due to Skype activating the FEC algorithm to counter any packet loss. In addition, when RSSI values were more than -88 dBm, Skype's sending rate decreased dramatically, even though there is plenty of bandwidth available in the link. This is because Skype tried to counteract this adaption and sent only the necessary data at a low and stable rate.

The measured results of Skype's packet size illustrate that Skype adapts its packet size as RSSI values decrease by increasing packet size in the signals between -60 dBm and -70 dBm by utilising the FEC algorithm. When the signal begins to decrease to less than -70 dBm, the packet size for all video sequences also decreases. Figure 4 below illustrates these findings.

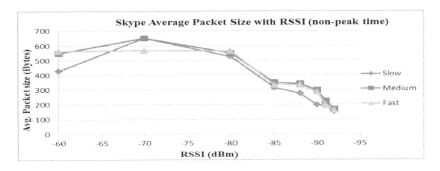

Figure 4: Skype average packet size for different RSSI values

In summary, when the signal strength reached -70 dBm, Skype increased its packet size in all videos. This can be explained as the result of Skype utilising the FEC algorithm in order to counter packet loss. On the other hand, when the signal started to weaken and decreased to less than -70 dBm, Skype counteracted this weakness by decreasing its packet size until reaching smaller packet sizes with a minimum RSSI value (-92 dBm).

4.2   Evaluating Skype video call quality

We also evaluated Skype video call quality under different RSSI values. This is of central importance in evaluating whether Skype can preserve its level of quality under different RSSI values. This was done by recording 24 degraded video calls over a smartphone device during the experiments. Then these 24 degraded videos were evaluated by 13 people with different backgrounds in terms of mean opinion scores (MOS). A subjective test website was designed using Surveygizmo Company website (Surveygizmo, 2013). Then, this evaluation website link was distributed to these people. They were asked to watch the degraded videos on the website and evaluate them according to the MOS scale by answering questions prepared for this purpose. In this evaluation, absolute category rating with hidden reference (ACR-HR) was used where the degraded videos were arranged randomly with an existence of a hidden reference video (ITU, 2009).

Table 1 illustrates the mapping of RSSI values to quality of experience achieved. The results demonstrate that there was a proportional decrease in the MOS scores as the RSSI values decreased. It also shows that RSSI values greater than around -70 provide good quality Skype video for all speeds of video motions. However, RSSI values less than about -88 dBm had poor quality. In addition, when RSSI values decreased, the percentage of accepting the Skype video quality is decreased especially with weak signals. We noticed that at RSSI values less than -90 dBm, the percentages reached 0% which indicates that subjects reject this quality as Skype video call.

In addition, these trends are similar to Mkwawa et al. (2012) results although they studied the mapping of RSSI values to QoE in VoIP applications over WLAN using voice, while in our findings the MOS scores obtained by subjective tests for different video calls, except for slow motion video calls with a RSSI between -80 dBm and -

90 dBm for which the average MOS was greater than 2.5. This could be because subjects did not seem to notice a big difference in the quality for slow motion video calls because the movements were concentrated in only a small area of the video.

RSSI (dBm)	Average MOS (all videos)	% accepting the quality as Skype video call (Slow)	% accepting the quality as Skype video call (medium)	% accepting the quality as Skype video call (fast)
-60	4.2	100%	100%	100%
-70	3.9	100%	100%	100%
-80	3.8	100%	85.70%	85.70%
-85	3.4	100%	71.40%	85.70%
-88	3.0	100%	57.10%	71.40%
-90	2.20	100%	14.30%	0%
-91	1.25	14.30%	0%	0%
-92	1.0	0%	0%	0%

Table 1: Mapping of RSSI to QoE and percentage for accepting the quality as Skype video call

In addition, the curve fitting technique was used to derive the relationship between average MOS scores and RSSI values for different motions in video calls. The following three graphs illustrate this relationship.

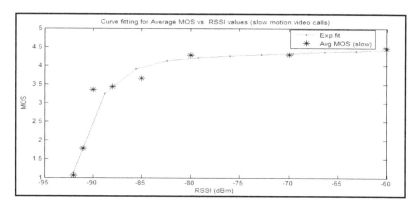

Figure 5: Curve fitting for average MOS vs. RSSI values (slow motion video calls)

Figure 5 demonstrates the exponential curve fitting derived for average MOS versus RSSI for slow motion video calls. The relationship between average MOS as f(x) and RSSI as (x) for slow motion video is described by the following exponential fitting equation: $f(x) = a*exp(b*x) + c*exp(d*x)$, where a= 5.075, b= 0.002181, c=-3.915e-015, and d= -0.3725. According to Mathworks_Fit (2013), Adjusted R-square statistic is generally the best indicator of the fit quality. It takes value less than or equal to 1. With a value closer to 1 indicating a better fit. For this curve fitting, adjusted R-square= 0.9049 which is very close to 1.

Figure 6 shows the polynomial curve fitting derived for average MOS versus RSSI for medium motion video calls. The relationship between average MOS as f(x) and RSSI as (x) for medium motion video is described by the following polynomial fitting equation: f(x) = p1*x^3 + p2*x^2 + p3*x + p4, where p1=0.0005175, p2=0.1139, p3=8.312, and p4= 204.8. For this curve fitting, adjusted R-square= 0.9689 which is very close to 1.

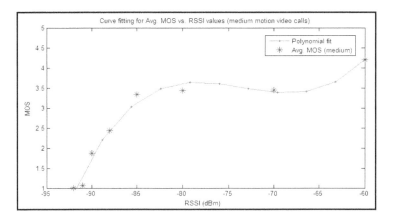

**Figure 6: Curve fitting for average MOS vs. RSSI values
(medium motion video calls)**

For fast motion video calls, Figure 7 shows the polynomial curve fitting equation derived for average MOS versus RSSI. The relationship between average MOS as f(x) and RSSI as (x) for video motion video is described by the following polynomial fitting equation: *f(x) = p1*x^3 + p2*x^2 + p3*x + p4*, where p1=0.0004358, p2=0.09398, p3=6.723, and p4= 163.2. In addition, adjusted R-square for this curve is = 0.8911.

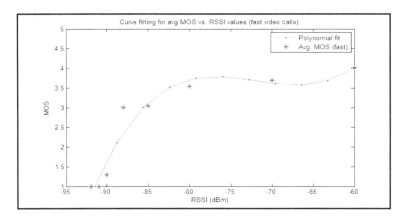

**Figure 7: Curve fitting for average MOS vs. RSSI values
(fast motion video calls)**

Moreover, 95% confidence intervals were calculated and plotted as shown in the following graphs. The bars with large intervals indicate less consistent results and small bars give an indication of more consistent results according to subject.

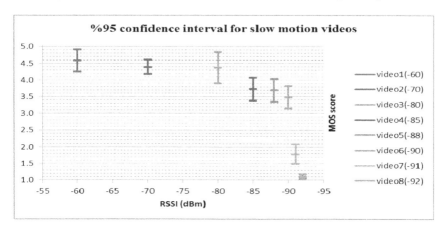

Figure 8: 95% confidence interval for MOS results for slow motion video calls

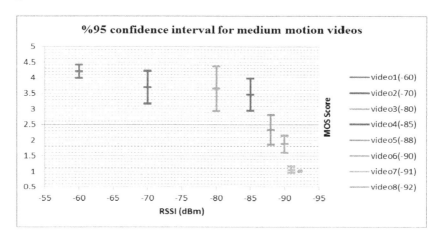

Figure 9: 95% confidence interval for MOS results for medium motion video calls

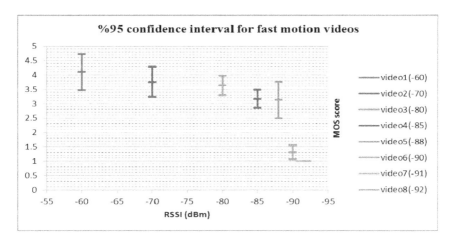

Figure 10: 95% confidence interval for MOS results for fast motion video calls

Slow motion video calls at a RSSI of -80 dBm have a larger confidence interval and RSSI -92 dBm has a smaller confidence interval. This indicates that subjects had more consistent results for video call quality with a RSSI of -92 dBm, which is the opposite for Skype video call quality at -80 dBm. The same findings were observed for medium video calls (figures 8 and 9).

For fast video calls (figure 10), subjects were more consistent at a RSSI of -91 dBm and -92 dBm. This is because the videos quality at these levels was very bad. On the other hand, video calls with a RSSI of -60 dBm and -88 dBm showed larger confidence intervals, which indicates that subjects seemed to give less consistent results for these two video calls.

5   Conclusion and future work

This paper has explored and evaluated Skype performance and quality under different RSSI values. Through extensive measurement, we have demonstrated that Skype responses towards different RSSI values. When signal strength between smartphone and router became weak, Skype reduced its sending rate and packet size significantly. Moreover, we have observed that most users accept Skype's quality when RSSI reaches -85 dBm or more, but they will not tolerate the quality when the RSSI decreases below that level.

For Future work, we aim to extend our work to different network infrastructures such as WiMax, UMTS, and 3G/4G networks and using several mobile devices with different platforms such as Android.

6   References

Boyaci, O., Forte, A. G. & Schulzrinne, H. (2009) Published. Performance of Video-Chat Applications under Congestion.   Multimedia, 2009. ISM '09. 11th IEEE International Symposium on, 14-16 Dec. 2009 2009. 213-218.

De Cicco, L., Mascolo, S. & Palmisano, V. (2011). Skype Video congestion control: An experimental investigation. Computer Networks, 55, 558-571.

Itu. (2009). P.910 : Subjective video quality assessment methods for multimedia applications [Online]. Available: http://www.itu.int/rec/T-REC-P.910-200804-I [Accessed 31 July 2013]

Manycam. (2013). ManyCam, The best free live studio & webcam effects software! [Online]. Available: http://manycam.com/ [Accessed 31 July 2013].

Mathworks_Fit. (2013). Evaluating Goodness of Fit [Online]. Available: http://www.mathworks.co.uk/help/curvefit/evaluating-goodness-of-fit.html [Accessed 15 August 2013]

Mkwawa, I.-H., Jammeh, E. & Sun, L. (2012) Published. Mapping of Received Signal Strength Indicator to QoE in VoIP applications over wlan. Quality of Multimedia Experience (QoMEX), 2012 Fourth International Workshop on, 2012. IEEE, 156-157.

Surveygizmo. (2013). Video Mean Opinion Score (MOS) Test [Online]. Available: http://www.surveygizmo.com/s3/1298674/Video-Mean-Opinion-Score-MOS-Test [Accessed 2 August 2013]

Wififofum. (2013). WiFiFoFum, Do you require a bespoke customised surveying tool for your organisation? [Online]. Available: http://www.wififofum.net/downloads [Accessed 31 July 2013].

Xinggong, Z., Yang, X., Hao, H., Liu, Y., Zongming, G. & Yao, W. (2012) Published. Profiling Skype video calls: Rate control and video quality. INFOCOM, 2012 Proceedings IEEE, 25-30 March 2012 2012. 621-629.

Zhu, J. (2011) Published. On traffic characteristics and user experience of Skype video call. Quality of Service (IWQoS), 2011 IEEE 19th International Workshop on, 2011. IEEE, 1-3.

Improving Security Incident Responses for End-users

H.Al-Mahmood and M.Papadaki

Center for Security, Communications and Network Research,
Plymouth University, Plymouth, United Kingdom
e-mail: info@cscan.org

Abstract

The Internet has grown in size and reach recently, and the number of users surfing the Internet has also grown significantly.

In the meantime, the Internet has also become a major source of different types of malicious activity; for instance, hackers use the Internet to encourage end-users to engage with services offered by malicious websites, for example by offering free downloads. This paper conducted an online questionnaire to investigate 84 participants' online behaviour and responses to security incidents that they had encountered in the past.

This research found a gap between current end-user responses and the response recommended by security vendors and security specialists. The research also found that the younger participants were responding better than the older group, and that participants who rated themselves as being highly aware of the issues (having good or average knowledge and awareness about security threats) actually tended to overestimate their security awareness level.

Keywords

Security awareness, Improve end-user's security awareness, Proper responses to security incidents.

1   Introduction

Many end-users consider security issues as major obstacles to surfing the Internet, which may prevent a wide range of end-users from utilizing the various services available online, such as online bank account management, online shopping, and social networking.

The Internet has become available to different end-user categories because the associated technology has become cheap and easy to use. Users vary from high to low educated groups, young to retirement age; these categories tend to have different levels of knowledge about the latest security threats, which will affect the way they respond to such incidents when they occur.

Despite of the fact that the Internet provides useful services to different end-users categories, it is also the source of security threats that target online users, especially those with less experience of security threats. Many different scenarios are used by hackers to fool end-users and infect their computer systems. Major threats coming from the Internet including phishing activities and spam emails as techniques to encourage end-users to visit malicious websites or obtain sensitive information

(Cocca, 2004); Malware infections (for instance virus, worms and Trojans); spyware; (see APWG, 2012; Malware Info resources centre, 2009 and Microsoft Safety and Security Centre, 2012).

Users' awareness about such security threats can play a vital role in avoiding, handling or mitigating the consequences of being under attack from security threats. This paper will investigate how end-users have responded to security threats in the past and compare it to some standard responses recommended by specialist staff, websites or vendors (for instance, Microsoft Security Centre).

Section 2 will discuss the importance of the end-user's security awareness and how it helps them to avoid falling into the risky situation of improper responses to such threats. Section 3 will explain the past work in the field towards improving end-user security awareness. Section 4 of this research will discuss the results obtained from an online survey that invited about 250 participants, of which 84 respondents provided useable data, since some answers were not accurate or reliable. Of the considered responses, enquiries designed using Microsoft Access 2010 was used to pick the answers that meet the criteria for each case study.

Section 5 will explain the conclusions that have been derived from the results and their analysis. Some suggestions will be listed to point out the major findings in this research.

2   The importance of security awareness

The term "Information Security Awareness" is used to indicate the state where end-users working at companies and organizations are aware of their information security responsibilities.

Improved security awareness should reduce faults and security incidents, and maximise the efficiency of security procedures from the user perspective (Siponen, 2000).

Human error and ignorance (not malicious intent) are the main reasons for most security incidents in the workplace. It is recommended to put significant effort into education improving workers' awareness in order to reduce these occurrences.

"The human element is the largest security risk in any organization," says Stephen Scharf, CISO at Experian and the former CSO of Bloomberg (Kaplan, 2010).

The Information Risk Executive Council (IREC) report (Kaplan, D., 2010) showed that 150 of its CISO members ranked "employee carelessness" as the top threat to enterprises in 2010.

3   Literature review

Talib *et al.* (2010) have carried out a survey to investigate the use, knowledge and practice relationships between home and the workplace. The study aimed to identify the learning approaches for end-users in both environments, to make a comparison between learning schemes in both places, and to investigate the possibility of transferring experience between environments.

The study employed a quantitative method to collect data from 330 surveyed participants, aiming to establish the general level of security knowledge for participants, how they improved their security skills, whether they were trained at work or somewhere else, and how efficient that training was. In addition, the project scrutinized the relation between security information obtained at home and in the workplace, and sought users' preferences for respective learning styles.

The main questions put to participants to investigate their knowledge concerned:

1- Their information security awareness.

2- Their practice at work, particularly the main source for their security information.

3- The sources they have used at home to develop their information security awareness, and the frequency with which they undertake learning.

The study concluded that generally participants who have trained showed high levels of security awareness in different areas. It also showed that the training provided by organizations or workplaces is well structured and more useful than the home learning style. In contrast, learning at home gives users more choices of security issues to learn about.

Further, learning provided by the workplace is more credible and focused on important aspects of awareness; unfortunately only about a third of organizations have a training programme in place.

Johnston et al. (2007) examined users' knowledge of certain kinds of malware. The aim of the study was to investigate users' awareness of malware that may affect the IT user. The survey included about 210 members of faculty and students from three higher institutes in different states in the USA, and IT staff. Most of the participants had experience in the Windows environment rather than operating Unix OS.

The study found that users are less knowledgeable about rootkit, compared to their experience with viruses and spyware (16.2% of users had heard about rootkit malware, compared to approximately 99.5% having had experience with viruses).

Results showed that the lower levels of awareness and experience about the rootkit have a number of causes.

The study suggested some recommendations for users to minimize rootkit malware's effects on their computers, such as intrusion detection and intrusion prevention systems. The study also recommended using antimalware utilities. Another important countermeasure is to keep all antimalware software updated, while educating users about the techniques used to install rootkit and increasing awareness about malicious websites.

The article entitled 'Global security awareness varies widely' published in SC magazine (2010), discussed a survey of 1450 participants from seven countries, and showed that there are different levels of awareness about different types of malware. Contrasting degrees of awareness of malware, both within the same country and across different countries were found. For example, the study found 41% of British participants thought that poisoned search was serious, while 28% had zero knowledge about it. As an example of variations for different countries, participants from Germany and Malaysia (77%, and 73% respectively) expressed greater concerns about privacy online, compared to Swedes and Finns (42% and 36% respectively). The study did not discuss why there are different levels of awareness and what the factors might be that could improve general awareness.

4   Results and analysis

In this section, the research will discuss several issues depending on results obtained from participants' answers, such as adopting security tools, whether end-users have one or more of these tools, the relation between the user's knowledge and the way they response to security threats. End-user estimates of their own level of awareness toward security threats and other findings will be discussed, such as unfamiliarity with common security threats or mechanism used by threats to spread across the end-user's computer system.

4.1   End-user's awareness categories

The research investigates end-users' familiarity with some popular security threats and how they rate their awareness of such security threats. Two major categories have been created for participants, in addition to a small group of experts. The first category consists of participants who believed they have average or good awareness level about security threats; the rest are classified as having low level awareness as they answered 'low' or 'basic'. According to this classification, the high awareness category consists of 66 out 84 of total participants, compared to 12 out of 84 participants for the basic level.

Regarding the high awareness category, results showed that approximately 41% of participants who ranked themselves as highly aware were not familiar with key logger spyware; approximately 60% had no idea about phishing activity. In contrast, 92% of the same categories were aware of spam techniques. This result states that a significant number in the high awareness category are not familiar with some of top threats coming from the internet, though a significant number of this category are familiar with spam emails; this reflects the experience of users in terms of the amount of spam they receive regularly. See Figure 1

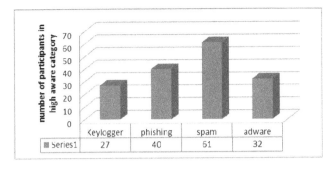

Figure 1: User's familiarity with security threats: high awareness category

5   Threats

This section will discuss the main results related to security tools such as antivirus and firewall. By looking at Table 1, one can tell that participants who already answered that they have antivirus installed and enabled reached 91% of participants. See Table 1.

Antivirus installed	Number of response out of (84)	Enabled always Out of 76	Updating status results for users installed and enabled AV			
			When available	daily	Weekly	Monthly
Yes	76	69	34	22	9	4

Table 1: Antivirus installation, activation and updating

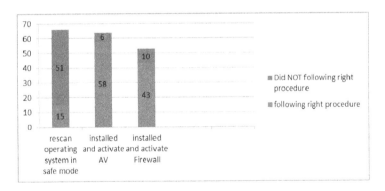

Figure 2: Correct behaviour and response to security threats

Looking at Figure 2 above, it is noticeable that a significant number of those in the high awareness category are not following the correct response or preparation as part of incident handling steps (Cook, 2000), so the research has found a gap between end-users' estimation of their level of awareness compare to the practical results. The second important result stated that participants who fall in the age group over 40 years old have several times undertaken the proper response and have better awareness about different security threats comparing to the other participants aged between 18-40 years old. See Figure 3

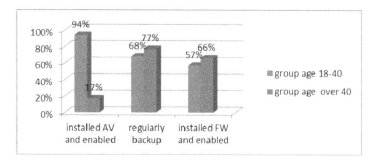

Figure 3: Relation between age group age and correct security behaviour

5.1   Credential management

Results for these questions showed that almost 73% of total participants have different usernames and passwords for different online accounts (group 1). Unfortunately, figures showed that users who claimed to change their credentials frequently only reached approximately 59% (this category consist of group 1 and user name for group of accounts). Frequently changing passwords makes compromised passwords less useful to the attacker. See Figure 4.

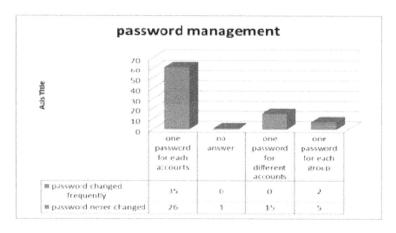

Figure 4: Credentials management

6   Conclusions and future work

Internet user numbers have risen significantly in the UK recently, and the rest of the world. Cheap costs and the simplicity of using the Internet have encouraged different categories of end-users to surf the Internet and utilize these services. However, security threats are still considered as major obstacles for a significant number of users.

This research has investigated many issues related to end-users' awareness about security threats that can come from using the Internet, and found some results as listed below:

1-The research investigated the relation between the age group of participants, and their past behaviour and responses to certain security threats. It was found that the group aged over 40 years old always gave better results compared to the younger group aged 18-40 years.

2-The second interesting finding was the overestimation of participants as end-users of their level of security skills and awareness. The majority in this category have in the past NOT responded properly to security incidents, in addition to showing poor knowledge about some popular types of threats, or failing to recognise infection mechanisms.

The research suggests designing a specific learning program to encourage younger people to improve their knowledge about security threats, which will improve the response of those in this category to security incidents. In addition, by encouraging end-users to update their general knowledge about current and famous security threats, and the proper response to each of them, this process will keep individuals up-to-date and familiar with recent security threats, rather than risk them missing or underestimating current threats.

7   References

APWG   (2012)   *Phishing   Activity   Trends   Report   1Q212*.   Available   at: http://docs.apwg.org/reports/apwg_trends_report_q1_2012.pdf (Accessed: 13 August 2012).

Cocca, P. (2004) *Email Security Threats*. Available at: http://www.sans.org/reading_room/ whitepapers/email/email-security-threats_1540. (Accessed: 13 November 2012)

Cook,   C   (2000)   *An   Introduction   to   Incident   Handling*.   Available   at: http://www.symantec.com/connect/articles/introduction-incident-handling.   (Accessed: 27 October 2012)

Johnston, A. C, Schmidt, M. B. Arnett, K. P and Thomas J (2007) 'Getting to the Root of the Problem' *Journal of Internet Commerce* , 6 (1), pp 1-12.

Kaplan,   D.   (2010)   *Weakest   link: End-user   education.*   Available   at: http://www.scmagazine.com/weakest-link-end-user-education/article/161685/.   (Accessed: 16 December 2012)

Malware   Info   resources   centre   (2009)   *Fighting   malware   injection.*   Available   at: http://www.malware-info.com/mal_faq_inject.html. (Accessed: 17November 2012)

Microsoft safety and security Centre (2012) PC Security: *How to prevent spyware*. Available at: http://www.microsoft.com/security/pc-security/spyware-prevent.aspx   (Accessed: 24   July 2012).

SC Magazine (2010), 'Global security awareness varies widely'. *SC Magazine: For IT Security Professionals* Nov/Dec2010, pp13.

Siponen, M. T., (2000) *A conceptual foundation for organizational information security awareness*. Information Management & Computer Security [Online], 8(1), pp. 31 – 41. Available at: http://www.emeraldinsight.com/journals.htm?articleid=862758&show=abstract (Accessed: 28 May 2012).

Talib, S., Clarke, N. L., and Furnell, S. M. (2010) 'An Analysis of Information Security Awareness within Home and Work Environments', *ARES '10 International Conference on Availability, Reliability, and Security.*, pp196 – 203.

Effect of Type of Policy on Moral Judgement and Attitude towards Information Security Behaviour: the Moderating Effect of Individualism and Collectivism

S.Alwatban and N.L.Clarke

Centre for Security, Communications and Network Research,
Plymouth University, Plymouth, United Kingdom
e-mail: info@cscan.org

Abstract

The importance of information security in any organisational environment is crucial e.g. personal details; data and confidential information can be easily compromised with poor awareness. The main aim of this research is to study people's awareness of information security. It is assumed that the type of policy adopted by an organisation and people's type of life philosophy will determine their awareness about information security. Particularly the researcher was interested on whether or not the type of policy (receiving Reward vs. Punishment) will have an effect on participants' awareness and whether or not the life philosophy will have an effect (Individualistic vs. Collectivistic) on their awareness. Security awareness was measured based on four main variables i.e. Moral behaviour, Behavioural Intention, Support of Policy and Trust in the university. By a questionnaire, as a data-gathering tool, 61 participants (Students of Plymouth University) took part in the study using convenience-sampling method. Using SPSS carried out using a MANOVA test (Multiple Analysis of Variance), the results showed participants who received the reward policy showed a significantly better moral behaviour regarding information security; however this difference was not observed in other dimensions i.e. behavioural intention, support of policy and trust in the university. Furthermore it was found that the collectivistic participants showed better behavioural intention to follow information security. Other results showed that both factors, when combined together, lead to a significant interaction with regard to moral behaviour, behavioural intention and students support of the policy. The effect of demographic variables such as gender, age, ethnicity and education were also tested. The results have made a significant contribution in the field of information security showing the psychological factors such as policy type and life philosophy should be considered highly in attempts to improve information security.

Keywords

Information Security Awareness, Culture, Individualism, Collectivism, Policy, Punishment and Reward schemes.

1 Introduction

A few decades ago, computers were first introduced as individual machines to store small amount of information and do some basic calculations. These machines were very large which made it difficult for them to be accommodated in homes. Therefore, they only existed in industries and on business premises. Also, they were so expensive that not any user could obtain any of them. Security issue was not a big issue at that time. Only physical access authentication was required in order to secure a standalone computer (Thomson and Solms 1998). Security engineers had to be aware of most natural threats such as earthquakes, floods, or fires (Thomson and Solms 1998). However, in comparison to a few years ago, prices of technical devices are fairly affordable these days. Moreover, the technology is getting smaller and smarter. As a consequence, the number of portable and desktop computers has considerably increased. They can be found literally everywhere; laboratories, homes, offices, banks, garages, and restaurants. Computers have invaded homes and they have become essential parts of daily activities. In addition, the fact that vast amount of information pertaining to our private lives, as well as sensitive data such as bank and medical details, makes information technology vulnerable to attack. In fact, breaches in information security are on the rise, despite much money and managerial effort being invested in maintaining this security.

To achieve goals of successful information security (the prevention of unauthorised access, use, disclosure, disruption, modification, or destruction) much hardware- and software- based securities have been employed by both organisations and individuals. However, the nature and risks of security breaches are ever evolving in such a way as to elude many technology-based solutions. In addition, human error is responsible for enabling the majority of security breaches. It is thus apparent that the solution lies in the hands of users and their awareness of information security. However, instigating awareness is not always enough to bring about behavioural changes. Developing reward schemes for incentivising those that follow information security policies may encourage greater cooperation, as may developing schemes to punish those that fail to follow proper security protocols. However, response to punishment and/ or reward schemes may be culturally influenced and may be mediated by the degree of individualism or collectivism that characterises a certain culture. Universities are organisations where information awareness is particularly important owing to the importance of information technology in education. In addition, students may be low in security awareness and compliance.

The importance of security issues has generated a wealth of research on information security, at individual, organisational and cross-cultural levels. However, the majority of research has concentrated on the organisational level, examining information security in different institutions such as law enforcement and government. In addition, research on an individual level has also been on the rise, examining use of coping mechanisms to reduce threats and adoption of security technologies, such as anti-spyware programs, as well as the protective role of user information security awareness (Liang & Xue, 2009). Cross-cultural research is needed in order to behaviours the differences in information security behaviour across cultures and why and how these differences arise. In addition, culture may affect moral judgement and attitudes arising due to information technology policies and any reward incentives or punishment schemes developed to enforce information security behaviour. The degree of individualism / collectivism of a culture seems to be very likely to interplay with awareness of information security issues as well as compliance with information security issues. The degree of individualism / collectivism in a society will also influence the extent to which reward or punishment schemes are successful in enhancing compliance with information security policies and guidelines.

This proposed study will investigate information security in Plymouth University, in the context of their information security policies. The mediating effect of the different cultures, in terms of their degree of individualism and collectivism of the two cultures and how this effects moral judgement, attitude, and response to reward or punishment schemes will also be examined.

2 Literature Review

2.1 Information Security

Computers have become a crucial part of our lives. They are used by individuals for a vast array of things, from socialising, to buying and selling and Internet banking. Needless to say, computer and Internet use by people world-wide is extensive. As a consequence, the occurrence of cybercrimes has also rapidly increased. In addition, as people spend increased amounts of time on the Internet, the possibility of chancing upon a threat or becoming victim to a cybercrime is also much increased. Nowadays, the majority of information kept by organisations is in electronic form. This information is managed and processed using information systems and is communicated expansively over private networks, as well as over the Internet. In reality, risks associated with information security are a critical challenge for organisations, given that these risks are detrimental to the operation of organisations and that the consequences can be dire and include loss of money and corporate liability (Cavusoglu, & Raghunathan, 2004). Evidence suggests that breaches in information security are on the rise (Symantec 2009) and in many organisations guaranteeing security of information security is one of the main priorities for management (Ransbotham & Mitra, 2009).

2.2 Information Security Awareness

In actual fact, recent evidence suggests that the majority of information security breaches result from human error and that end users are often the weakest link in information security (Bilal *et al.*, 2011; Durgin, 2007). Thus, users may jeopardise information security due to their mistakes and general lack of information security awareness. Human errors include things like password mistakes, (such as using a weak password), downloading email attachments from unknown users, and ignoring security measures due to naivety concerning the reality of threats. Actions in the physical world, such as leaving important information showing on the desktop and walking away and leaving the computer open without logging off are also errors that may threaten information security. This weakness in security can be very harmful in terms of loss of money and privacy (Mainiwatts, 2007).

Information security awareness can be said to describe an individual's understanding of information security. This understanding is in terms of: the reality of risks and the threat that they pose; users' individual responsibilities and how an individuals' actions may influence information security (Bilal *et al.*, 2011). Millions of people world-wide are now internet users, and part of a digital world and computers play a pivotal role in their everyday lives. These people, that originate from hundreds of countries, cultures and backgrounds, are now interconnected, along with their digital information systems and networks. This makes them very vulnerable to a wide assortment of threats. This has created new security issues that have led to a wide variety of new guidelines being established. These new guidelines apply to users from all spheres and indicate that greater awareness and understanding is needed in order to establish a culture of security.

2.3   Behavioural issues: punishment and reward

In order to achieve greater compliance with information security measures it is important to have an understanding of what factors motivate users to comply with information security policies. This understanding will enable managers of information security to diagnose how weakness in information security may be solved using behavioural approaches. This can be described as 'security culture' and encompasses all socio-cultural actions that support technical information security measures.

Various policies of recompensing and sanctioning can be utilized in order to regulate users' social behaviours in information security. In the framework of information security this entails delivering punishments for violating security (Parker, 1999) and/ or rewarding observance (Kabay 2002; Parker, 1999). Such external incentives may influence information security behaviour because people may seek to be rewarded and seek to avoid being punished. Straub and Nance (1990) investigated how computer abuses could be detected. They suggested that organisations should employ punishment and that in series cases punishments should be as harsh as possible. Straub and Nance argued that this would deter other people from behaving in a similar manner. Mulder (2008) contended that punishment is a way to encourage people towards actions that are considered morally correct. On the other hand, other research findings suggest that reward may induce a greater degree of moral concern than punishment would (Greitemeyer & Kazemi, 2008).

This, taken together with the contradiction in research findings of whether punishment or reward is more effective, indicates that the effectiveness of punishment versus reward may in fact depend on the individual and whether they consider that co-operation is a voluntary behaviour or a moral obligation. This may, for example, be dependent on the individuals' social value orientation (Sattler & Kerr, 1991). Social value orientation may in fact be explained in terms of the moderating effect of individualism and collectivism. Much less attention, however, has been given to the effects of the levels of individualism and collectivism and the extent to which this can moderate the different effects of punishment and reward schemes.

2.4   Culture: the moderating effect of individualism/ collectivism

People from different cultures vary significantly in the way that they see themselves and the world, and the relationship between the two (Markus & Kitayama, 1991). For example a study of spyware awareness and spyware knowledge found that culture was an influencing factor. In comparative study by Dinev and colleagues (2009) information technology users' in Korea and the United States were compared. Clear differences were found in the relationship between subjective norms and individuals' use of antispyware technology, spyware awareness, and attitude to spyware In a further study it was found that computer users in the United States perceived themselves as more aware of threats of viruses and anti-spyware securities than Chinese computer users (Schmidt, *et al* 2008). This suggests that belonging to each of the two distinct cultures had a major influence on the differences in awareness of information threats and securities.

Cultures can be defined along a scale from individualistic to collectivist and this has been considered to be the most important factor in explaining the difference between cultures (Triandis, 2001). Significant variation between Western and Eastern cultures in terms of individualism has been observed (Markus & Kitayama, 1991). However, usually, within a specified culture, individuals differ significantly in the extent to which they are representative of the individualistic or collectivist nature of the culture (Triandis, 1989). Individualism is defined by self-reliance, competiveness and aggressive creativity and collective goals are subsumed under individual goals. Collectivism, by contrast, is characterised by an emphasis on group or community. Collectivistic people regard the self as a collective feature, taking into account widely the needs of others. Values and beliefs are derived from the group and group interests and goals take precedence over individual ones. The individual is intrinsically linked to others and not separate from them. Social norms and duty are defined by the group, rather than pleasure seeking (Hofstede *et al.*, 1991). In terms of awareness, individualist societies place more emphasis on the importance of privacy and thus have greater awareness and knowledge of security issues. By contrast, collectivist cultures are characterised by unified communities and very often exist in huge family systems making them generally less used to having privacy (Sung, 2004).

Further, control is also influenced by the degree of individualism/collectivism of a given culture. Individualistic cultures generally are orientated towards primary control whilst collectivistic cultures emphasise secondary control (Eisenberg, 1999). Primary control can be described as the drive to influence and control the existing reality. This entails manipulating existing realities by striving to shape people, behaviours, objects and/or circumstances. By contrast, secondary control accommodates the current reality by instead aspiring to change the internal self, rather than external features. This involves swaying self-expectations, ambitions, viewpoints, outlook, and attributions (Eisenberg, 1999; Weisz *et al.*, 1984). A cultures primary form of control may moderate the effect of reward or punishment policies since; individualists (primary controllers) endeavour to manipulate external realities to fit the internal self, whilst conversely collectivists (secondary controllers) emphasise the altering of the self to adapt to the external realities.

3 Methodology

Since the current research is following the positivist research paradigm the researcher concluded that the most suitable research method would be the Quantitative method. It will allow the researcher to generate quantitative data to confirm or reject the withdrawn hypotheses.

3.1   A questionnaire

A questionnaire is a research instrument (type of survey) that includes a set of questions that have a quantitative nature of answers. All questions are scored based on numbers reflecting a meaning (e.g. 5-points likert scale ranging from 1= strongly disagree to 5=strongly agree). Questionnaires are considered one of the most followed research instruments in quantitative research that follow the positivist research paradigm. Questionnaires generally include closed-ended questions where the participant is asked to choose from a given category. Questionnaire as a quantitative research instrument has many advantages over qualitative research instruments (e.g. Interviews)… a questionnaire enables the researcher to quantify for a specific phenomenon, to gain a mathematical understanding of its outcomes and generalise the outcomes from the sample to the bigger population. It is considered a cost effective data-gathering tool that allows access to high number of participants in a short space of time. On the other hand questionnaires could have disadvantages in that they offer abstract or brief information/answers compared to a method like Interviews where participants are allowed to offer in-depth answers. For the purpose of this research a questionnaire is considered the best data-gathering tool when considering the factors such as Time, the type of information to be gathered, and the ability to accept or reject the main research hypotheses. Questionnaires are suitable for explaining relationships between factors as well as cause and effect which are the essence of the hypotheses (Saunders *et al.*, 2007). Following a questionnaire data gathering too the designed questionnaire in this study was divided into Six Parts:

Information Sheet: this part of the questionnaire provides the participants brief information about the topic under research while highlighting that the participation is completely voluntary and they are allowed to withdraw from participation at any given time.

Demographic Data: this part enquires about the general background information about the participants e.g. their Gender, Age, Nationality (ethnicity), education in Plymouth University and education level.

Life Philosophy: This part of the questionnaire is adopted from Triandis (1996), it enquires about participants life philosophy, mainly it looks at two aspects Individualism and Collectivism. The individualism is measured through 8 questions that are answered on a 7-points Likert Scale (1=Strongly disagree, 2=Disagree, 3=Slightly disagree, 4=Neither agree nor disagree, 5= Slightly agree, 6=Agree, 7= Strongly agree). Overall these questions aim to find out if the participant is considered individualistic or not.

Policy type: in this part participants are asked to read an article depicting either a Reward or Punishment Policy relating to the topic of information security awareness at Plymouth University. The reward policy article talks about the paln of the Plymouth University to improve the information security awareness amongst students and that the proposed measures include an initiative to financially reward students who conform to the security policy. However in the Punishment policy student are financially punished if they do not conform to the security policy. They are two separate articles and participants were either provided with the Reward policy article or the Punishment policy and not both.

Opinions about the Policy: after reading either of the policy article participants were asked to rate their opinions and acceptance about general aspects of online information security in Plymouth University. This questionnaire was designed by the researcher based on his understanding of the topic, it consists of 20 items which are categorised under Four categories and answered on a 7-points Likert agreement scale (1=strongly disagree, 7=strongly agree) the categories are as follows:

1- Moral Behaviour: this part includes 4 statements talking about the morality of information security after reading the Reward or the Punishment policy.
2- Behavioural Intention: this part includes 12 statements enquiring about participants' intention to conform with the policies of information security and increase their own awareness.
3- Support of Policy: the support policy includes items regarding the extent to which participants are supporting the implemented policy whether it is Reward or Punishment, it includes 3 items.
4- Trust in the University: finally there was one question asking on the extent to which the participants trust or think that the university takes the best interest for the students at heart.

Final statement: this part of the questionnaire thanked participants for their participation and completion of the questionnaire; it included the main purposes of the study and also included the researcher's details if any questions need to be raised with regard to the questionnaire and the research as a whole.

3.2 Procedure

After determining the research data collection tool and finalising the questionnaire the researcher made copies of the questionnaires (Reward and Punishment). The researcher had planned to use online Questionnaire (Monkeysurvey.com) however failure to recruit participants let to a change in approach. Participants were approached in person in the university Campus (Plymouth University). The researcher followed Convenience sampling method where he approached participants based on their availability in the university and their willingness to participate. Upon his approach of the participants the researcher introduced himself and what is his research about and whether they are willing to take part, participant who declined volunteering where thanked and those who accepted participation where given a copy of the questionnaire to read and were told that it would take about 15 minutes to fill in the questionnaire.

4 Result

A number of hypotheses were determined in this research involving two main Independent Variables (the manipulated variables) and a number of Dependent variables (the variables measured). The independent variable in concern are the Type of Policy (Reward vs. Punishment) and the Life Philosophy (Individualistic vs. Collectivistic), whereas the main dependent variables of concern are Moral Behaviour (MB), Behavioural Intention (BI or attitude), Support of policy and Trust of Plymouth university. Hence the most suitable Parametric test to be conducted is a MANOVA test which tests the main effects of each independent variable on each dependent variable and it also tests whether an significant interaction exists between the two independent variable with regard to each dependent variable. The significance of the results as explained earlier will be determined based on an alpha level of 5%, probabilities below this value are considered of significant effect. Using SPSS the data was examined following suitable instructions of MANOVA, the following analysis will examine the main effects of each independent variable and the interaction effect.

4.1   Main effect of Policy: Reward vs. Punishment

Policy type (reward and punishment) appeared to have a significant main effect on just one of the dependents variables which is the Moral Behaviour (behavioural concern), $F(1,57)=12.17$, $p=0.000$. the results were very significant at $p=0.001$ reflecting that there is a chance of less than 0.1% of the results being down to chance and not a result of the independent variable. Based on the mean scores it is evident that overall (regardless of life philosophy) participants who received the reward scheme/policy had a better and more positive Moral behaviour (M=6.03) compared to participants who received the punishment policy (M=5.25). However from the results of both it is evident that both groups had positive moral behaviour, both means were above the middle point of 4 (either agree or disagree).

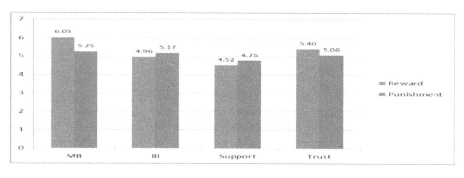

Figure 1: Shows the mean scores of the dependent variables based on policy type

4.2   Life philosophy effect: Individualistic vs. collectivistic

Different from the previous section this one looks at the main effect of the life philosophy (Individualistic and collectivistic) on the four dependent variables. To start with it was evident from the MANOVA test that the life philosophy has no significant main effect on the Moral Behaviour, $F(1,57)=2.41$, $p=0.159$. By looking at the mean scores it was shown that the Collectivistic group showed a slightly higher means score (M=5.71) compared to the individualistic group (M=5.58), however the difference was not significant enough to result in significant difference. Both means showed positive agreement.

The life philosophy showed a significant main effect on the Behavioural Intention of participants, $F(1,57)=12.44$, $p=0.001$. The results were significant at 1% showing that there is a chance of less than 1% of the results being down to chance. By looking at the mean scores it was clear that the collectivistic group of participants had a significantly higher and more positive mean (M=5.28) compared to the individualistic group (M=4.76), however both show a positive agreement overall.

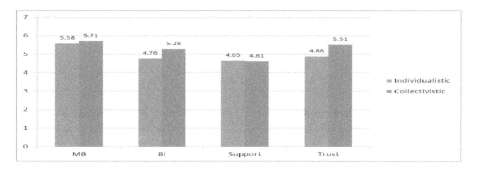

Figure 2: Shows the mean scores of the dependent variables based on life philosophy

4.3   Interaction effect: Policy X Philosophy

Different from the above two sections here the interaction between the Policy type and the Life Philosophy Type is measured i.e. the interaction aims to find whether the scores in each of the dependent variables change as a function of the interaction between both independent variables.

A significant interaction effect was found between both variables when looking at the Moral behaviour, F(1,57)=15.34, p=0.000. By looking at Figure 3 It can be seen that individualistic group of participants had higher moral behaviour (M=6.26) in the reward policy compared to the collectivistic group (M=5.82), however the opposite happened in the punishment policy where the collectivistic group(M=5.61) had a higher mean score in moral behaviour compared to the individualistic group (M=4.65).

A significant interaction effect was found when considering the Behavioural Intention, F(1,57)=8.04, p=0.006, Figure 4 shows that both groups, the individualistic (M=4.90) and the collectivistic (M=5.00) showed similar behavioural intention scores in the reward policy however when assessing the punishment condition the collectivistic group had a higher mean (M=5.54) compared to the individualistic group (M=4.58) who showed a decreased mean score.

Also a significant interaction effect was found when measuring for the Support of policy, F(1,57)=46.02, p=0.000. Figure 5 Illustrates that the in the reward policy the individualistic group had a higher mean score in the support of policy (M=5.22) compared to the collectivistic group (M=3.90), however when looking at the punishment policy the individualistic group (M=3.87) had a lower mean score compared to the collectivistic group (M=5.29).

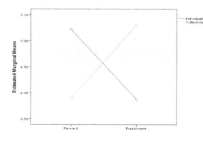

Figure 3: Interaction in moral behaviour

Figure 4: Interaction in behavioural intention

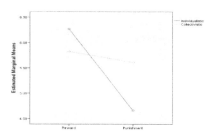
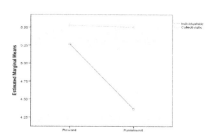

Figure 5: Interaction in support of policy

Figure 6: Interaction in trust in the university

4.4   Ethnicity effect: European, Asian-oriental, Middle-Eastern

Participants where grouped based on their ethnicity into three groups (Asian-Oriental, Middle Eastern and European participants) this section aims to find out whether the ethnicity has a significant effect on participants Moral Behaviour, Behavioural Intention, Support and Trust. To do so the researcher followed a One Way Analysis of Variance (ANOVA), this is a parametric test that aims to find the difference between three independent groups (i.e. the effect of an independent variable of three levels or more). The results of this tests showed that the ethnicity has a significant effect on participants Support of policy $F_{(2,58)}=3.36$, $p=0.041$, the results are significant at $p<0.05$. When observing the mean scores between group it was evident that the European participants (M=5.01) had the highest support of policy Compared to the Middle-Eastern (M=4.51) and the Asian-Oriental Group (M=4.28). Furthermore a Post-hoc test (Bonferroni) was conducted to find the difference between any two of the groups, it was found that the European group had a mean score which was significantly different from the Asian-Oriental group (p=0.041), no significant difference was found between the Middle eastern and the European (p=0.426) and between the middle-eastern and the Asian-Oriental group (p=1.00).

A significant effect was found for the ethnicity on the participants level of Trust in the Plymouth university, $F_{(2,58)}=6.738$, $p=0.002$. The mean scores showed that again the European participants had the highest level of trust in the university

(M=5.84) compared to the Middle-eastern (M=5.61) and the Asian-Oriental (M=4.39). Using a Bonferroni Post-hoc test it was shown that there is a significant difference between the European and the Asian-Oriental group of participants (p=0.003), also between the Middle-eastern and the Asian-Oriental (p=0.041). No difference was found between the European and the Middle Eastern group of participants (p=1.00).

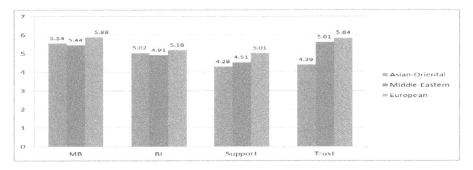

Figure 7: The mean scores of the dependent variables based on the ethnicity

4.5 Gender Effect: Male Female

Gender as an independent variable has two levels (Male and Female); the purpose of this section is to report whether or not the gender has any significant effect on the dependent variables (Moral Behavioural, Behavioural Intention, Support and Trust). A suitable test here would be the Independent Samples t-test which assesses the effect of an independent variable of two levels (the difference between two groups) with regard to the given dependent variables. The output of the t-test showed that the Levene's Test of Equality assumed unequal variances (F=9.16, p=0.004) following this assumption it was shown the results of the t-test showed a significant effect of gender on the level of Trust participants have, the Female group (M=6.06) a significantly higher mean compared to the Male group (M=4.95), the results were significant at t(59)=3.09, p=0.004.

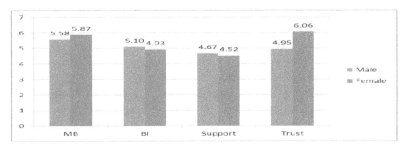

Figure 8: the average scores of the dependent variables based on gender

5 Conclusion & Future Work

The general aim of the study was to examine awareness of information security (moral behaviour, behavioural intention, support of policy and trust in The Plymouth university) in relation to the policy type (reward vs. punishment) and the life philosophy (individualistic vs. collectivistic). The risks associated with information security are a critical challenge for organisations (Cavusoglu, & Raghunathan, 2004). Hence the importance of the information security in any organisation is immense and when considering the academic environment i.e. universities it is important that students possess good level of awareness in information security and also there is an urgent to understand factors that might moderate or compromise such awareness. To investigate the main aim of this research the current study developed a number of hypothesises. The hypotheses were all tested based on data generated from a questionnaire partially developed by Triandis (1996) and partially developed by the researcher based on previous literature. By following suitable statistical tests and using SPSS the researcher examined all hypotheses some of which were accepted and others were rejected. Firstly the researcher was concerned on whether the type of policy adopted by the participants (reward or punishment) has an effect on participants' level of awareness in information security/ in doing so it was evident that the policy type had a significant effect on participants' Moral behaviour where the reward scheme led to a significantly higher score of moral behaviour with regard to information security. No significant effect of policy type was found on behavioural intention, support of policy and trust in the university.

Furthermore the researcher was interested in finding whether the life philosophy (individualistic vs. collectivistic) has any impact on the information security awareness. It was found that it had a significant impact on the behavioural intention with regard to information security favouring the collectivistic participants. The interaction between life philosophy and the policy type was also measured, it was found that there is a significant interaction effect between the policy type and the life philosophy when considering moral behaviour, behavioural intention and students support of the policy.

The researcher considered the effect of other factors such as ethnicity, gender, age and education. Ethnicity showed a significant effect on the support of the policy (favouring European students) and trust in Plymouth University (favouring the European students).

The research Implication could be considered by universities seeking to reinforce information security policies, huge importance should be placed on policy scheme and the type of life philosophy adopted by students. It should be noted that overall the universities should adopt different policies to suit the different life philosophies. The study can be criticised in different aspects and had a number of research limitations. This is a small scale study involving 61 participants from Plymouth University hence it is problematic to generalise the outcomes of the study to the bigger population. Although the researcher aimed to have the same number of participants in each of the policy schemes that did not work out due to shortage in participants and lack of time. Furthermore the researcher talked about the general awareness of the information security touching on moral behaviour, behavioural intention, support of policy and trust in Plymouth University. Such variables were measured using different number of items/questions (e.g. support had three items and trust of university was presented by one item), the questionnaire did not include the type of information security and was based on online information security mainly as most universities rely heavily on the use of e-learning or virtual learning through the use of computers. However there must be a need to explore different types of information securities and the type of threats and errors that might lead to the compromise of privacy and see students' awareness of them.

It could be recommended in future research that information security should be carefully defined in the context of academia while highlighting the possible threats and factors that compromise the security and privacy. Such factors should be surveyed among participants. Secondly it is recommended that future research should involve a significantly higher number of participants across all conditions and categories, such recommendation leads to a better generalizability and a better understanding of information security. Furthermore it could be helpful to see whether computer literacy in general has any impact on students' awareness of information security (because universities nowadays are involving a lot of computer use). Although the questionnaire have achieved content validity (measuring what it is supposed to measure) and a high reliability (measuring for the same thing) there is a still more need to incorporate higher number of items (especially when testing for trust and support of policy). Furthermore ethnicity as and factor affecting awareness should be examined in more details. Taking into consideration such aspects will improve future research and provide more reliable outcomes.

6 References

Bilal, K. Khaled, A. Syed, I Nabi and Muhammad, K. (2011). Effectiveness of information security awareness methods based on psychological theories. *African Journal of Business Management*. 5 (26), 10862-10868.

Cavusoglu, H., and Raghunathan, S (2004) "Economics of IT Security Management: Four Improvements to Current Security Practices," *Communications of the Association for Information Systems* (14), pp. 65-75.

Cavusoglu, H., and Raghunathan, S (2004) "Economics of IT Security Management: Four Improvements to Current Security Practices," Communications of the Association for Information Systems (14), pp. 65-75.

Cavusoglu, H., Son, J.-Y., and Benbasat, I. (2009). "Information Security Control Resources in Organizations: A Multidimensional View and Their Key Drivers," *working paper, Sauder School of Business*, University of British Columbia.

Dinev, T., Goo, J., Hu, Q., and Nam, K. (2009)"User Behaviour towards Protective Information Technologies: The Role of National Cultural Differences," *Information Systems Journal*, Vol. 19. No. 4, pp. 391-412.

Eisenberg, J. (1999). How Individualism-Collectivism Moderates the Effects of Rewards on Creativity and Innovation: A Comparative Review of Practices in Japan and the US. *Creativity and Innovation Management*, 8(4), 251-261.

Greitemeyer, T., & Kazemi, E. (2008). Asymmetrical consequences of behavioral change through reward and punishment. *European Journal of Social Psychology*, 38, 246-259. doi: 10.1002/ejsp.

Kabay ME (2002) Using Social Psychology to Implement Security Policies. 4th edition. John Wiley & Sons, Inc., USA,32.1-32.16.

Korovessi.P (2011) " Information Security Awareness in Academia,". *International Journal of Knowledge Society Research.* 2(4), pp. 1-7

Liang, H. and Xue Y. (2009) "Avoidance of Information Technology Threats: A Theoretical Perspective," *MIS Quarterly,* Vol. 33, No 1, pp. 71-90

Mainiwatts, Marketing Group (2007), "World internet Usage Statistics News and Population Stats", Available at: http://www.internetworldstats.com/stats.htm. (Accessed 3 Joan 2013).

Markus. H.R., Kitayama.S. (1991) Culture and The Self: Implication for conation, emotion and motivation, *Psychological Review.* 98(2), 224-253.

Mulder, L. B. (2008). The difference between punishments and rewards in fostering moral concerns in social decision making. *Journal of Experimental Social Psychology,* 44(6), 1436-1443. doi: 10.1016/j.jesp.2008.06.004.

Ransbotham, S., and Mitra, S (2009) "Choice and Chance: A Conceptual Model of Paths to Information Security Compromise," *Information Systems Research* (20:1), pp.121-139.

Sattler, D. N., & Kerr, N. L. (1991). Might versus morality explored: Motivational and cognitive bases for social motives. *Journal of Personality and Social Psychology, 60*(5), 756-765.

Saunders, M., Lewis, P. and Thornhill, A. (2007). *Research methods for business students.* 4th ed. London: Prentice Hall.

Schmidt, M.B., Johnston A.C., Arnett, K.P., Chen, J.Q., and Li, S., (2008)"A Cross-Cultural Comparison of U.S. and Chinese Computer Security Awareness," *Journal of Global Information Management,* Vol. 16, No. 2, pp. 91-103

Straub, D. W., Nance, W. (1990) "Discovering and Disciplining Computer Abuse in Organization: A Field Study". *MIS Quarterly.* Vol. 14,No.1 pp.45-60.

Sung, S., (2004) "There is No Cyber Privacy (?)," *Digital Contents,* April, pp. 120-128.

Symantec (2009) "Symantec Internet Security Threat Report: Trends for 2008, Symantec Corporation, Cupertino, CA" Available at: http://eval.symantec.com/mktginfo/ enterprise/white_papers/bwhitepaper_exec_summary_internet_security_threat_report_xiv_04-2009.en-us.pdf. (Accessed: 17 Jan 2013).

Thomson, M. Solms, R (1998) " *Information security awareness: educating your users effectively",* IEEE journal, Vol. 6, Issue 4 Pages:167-173

Triandis, H.C., (1989) "The Self and Social Behaviour in Differing Cultural Contexts," *Psychological Review,* Vol. 96, No. 3.

Triandis, H.C., (2001) "Individualism-Collectivism and Personality," *Journal of Personality,* Vol. 69, No. 6, pp. 907-924.

Weisz, J. R., Rothbaum, F. M., & Blackburn, T. C. (1984). Standing out and standing in: The psychology of control in America and Japan. *American Psychologist, 39*(9), 955-969.

Investigating Perceptions of Risk
to Professional Reputation

R.Brett and S.Atkinson

Center for Security, Communications and Network Research,
Plymouth University, Plymouth, United Kingdom
e-mail: info@cscan.org

Abstract

Through an investigation into existing materials and tools available to help professionals manage their online identity and reputation, the literature was evolved to determine the main risks involved. By investigating the perceptions of the risks posed to professional reputation by the internet, it was possible to determine any gaps in the knowledge of a group in a specific profession. Consequently, by considering the possible mitigation steps which could be taken and the steps which are taken by this particular group, it was also possible to determine any gaps in knowledge thereof. Further, through the expansion of existing materials in combination with the shortfalls in knowledge determined with the group considered, it was possible to design and implement a support document aimed specifically at the particular profession of illustration and relating to the use of the internet for self-promotion.

Keywords

Professional reputation, cyber bullying, social networking, bullying, Internet, web 2.0

1   Introduction

As a consequence of the current state of the UK economy and the issues for employment this has brought about, more and more people are turning to self-employment in order to make a living. According to the Office of National Statistics, *"There are now 367,000 more people who are self-employed than there were in 2008... More than 200,000, or 60% of these, became self-employed between 2011 and 2012."* (Bachelor, 2013). This is especially relevant for young people and recent graduates, as there is such stiff competition when rare employment opportunities do arise.

In particular, those who are in the more creative professions (photography, illustration, graphic design, 3D design etc.) can find that working on a freelance basis is the best way to find success and earn a living. In order to become successful in these professions, it is vital to take advantage of the many promotional tools which the internet has to offer, be they social networks, blogging, websites or other sites such as online galleries. However, the use of these sites and the necessity to have an online presence can have many negative effects on professional reputation.

This research considers a group of illustration students, and aims to investigate their perceptions with regard to the risks which the internet poses to their professional identity and to consider what steps they take to mitigate these risks. Following an in-depth analysis of the materials already available to help mitigate these possible risks, the project then went on to produce support materials tailored to the needs of the participants in the study, in order to help them to deal with any risks to identity or professional reputation as best as they can.

2 Background: Online risks to individuals

In recent years, the internet and more specifically the use of social networks has become a part of everyday life for a large percentage of individuals. With this degree of information sharing and online presence come many new risks to individuals, especially when portraying themselves online. As social media grows in popularity, so does the level of risk associated with using it - people are sharing more and more information about themselves, which leaves them open to abuse and exploitation.

Most of the recent research into social media and the risks associated therein has been carried out with respect to the safety of children and young adults. There is now a whole generation of children who have grown up around computers and for whom technology is the norm. Extensive research is therefore being carried out into what risks the internet poses to them, and educational materials are being produced by projects including EU Kids Online (LSE, 2013) and the UK Safer Internet Council (UKSIC, 2013), in order to mitigate the harmful effects which come from these risks.

In a recent report following their multinational study, EU Kids Online (O'Neill et al, 2011) stated that the main risks in this area have been found to be those of contact with unknown others and exposure to harmful or sexual material. Also, to a lesser extent, cyber bullying, which is a subject also discussed in a paper by Stauffer (2012) and extensively in a book by Shariff (2008). Although the EU Kids Online survey found cyber bullying to be the least common risk to children, they also found that it was the most harmful or upsetting. In the context of risks to children, it is important to distinguish between risk and harm.

For adults in particular, the problem of online abuse is closely related to the idea of free speech and what you can openly say online. This is an area where professionals and businesses need to be especially careful, as some things said online cannot be easily retracted.

Another category of risk which has been found for users of social media is that of psychological issues, as social networking has been linked to depression and other mental health problems. There is even a suggestion of the possibility of becoming 'addicted' to social networking, as it becomes more and more a part of everyday life.

This idea of addiction or excessive use of social networking in particular has been investigated by authors including Kuss & Griffiths (2011) and Griffiths (2012) and was also touched upon in the EU Kids Online study by O'Neill et al (2011). This issue also ties in with the idea of "hyper-connectivity" as discussed in Government

Office for Science report on Future Identities (GOFS, 2012), which relates to the idea that the world is becoming a place where people are connected to the internet and to each other in some way or another at all times.

While adults are more likely to be able to control which sites they visit, and hence make their own decisions about what material they are exposed to, they have not necessarily been educated about online safety and hence are likely to make mistakes all the same. Therefore, materials are being created not just for children, but for parents, teachers and carers as well, to educate them on the risks in order to help both children and themselves.

The other main group of users for whom the risks of social media use are being investigated is business users. These risks are predominantly the same, including privacy issues, identity theft and cyber bullying, but also extend more into areas such as professional reputation management. This was the main area considered in this study.

3   Methodology

The main aim of the research carried out in this project was to produce a prototype support document to help a targeted audience to feel confident protecting their identity and reputation online. This began with a survey to ascertain the views of a group of established illustration professionals as well as students working towards a career in illustration. This gathered information on the group's perceptions of the risks posed to their professional identity by the Internet, as well as the methods used to mitigate these risks. Following the completion of this survey, it was possible to analyse the results in order to determine the main areas in which guidance was needed for this particular group and develop useful advice which could also be more widely utilised by those in the illustration profession.

The survey was distributed via email to a total of 106 potential participants including 6 lecturers, 46 third year students and 54 second year students. Having been online and collecting results for six weeks, the survey had a total of 24 responses. Three of these responses did not go beyond the consent stage. Of the remaining 21, there were 3 partial responses and 18 full responses. This gives an overall response rate of just under 20%.

There were five main sections to the questions asked:
- Demographic data
- Use of the internet for self-promotion
- Perceptions of risk
- Personal experiences of risk
- Mitigation steps taken

The data collected was then transferred to an Excel spread sheet, collated and analysed accordingly. Findings will be considered briefly for each section of survey questions in turn.

4   Findings

4.1   Section one: participant background/ demographic

The first section of the survey consisted of a number of personal questions to determine details of the demographic questioned and enable the results to be extrapolated to a larger audience. Firstly, the age and gender of participants was collected. Respondents were predominantly (67%) male. The highest number of responses came from the 18-29 age bracket (90%), with only 5% aged 40-49 and 5% aged 50-59. None of the respondents were in the 30-39 or 60+ age groups.

Participants were then asked to give their position at the university, which involved selecting whether they were a student or lecturer. In this case, the majority of participants were students, with only 5% of the total number of respondents listing themselves as 'tutor or lecturer'. Of the remaining student respondents, 70% were in their third year of study with the remaining 30% in their second year. This was expected as third years were still in term time when invited to complete the survey, whereas second years finished their term a lot earlier so a lower response rate was to be expected from this group. By determining in particular whether students' views vary between the second and third year of study, it should be possible to show whether any gaps in knowledge are filled in the third year of their course, when an emphasis is put on Internet promotion. Similarly, any differences can be determined between the knowledge of different age groups and genders.

After collecting general demographic data, the survey went on to consider what areas of the Internet participants use to promote themselves and their work.

4.2   Section two: Online presence.

Section two asked participants to give details relating to their online presence and Internet usage. This section began by finding out which methods of online self-promotion participants used. They were asked to select as many as applied from the given list. It was found that 90% had a website and 80% had a blog, making these the most popular methods used. 75% of respondents had both of these. Only 40% of respondents use Facebook for professional reasons and, interestingly, the same number use Twitter (40%). This is surprising as, in general, Facebook is seen as the more popular social network, and has more users around the world. (Smith, 2013), therefore it was expected that Facebook would be used more.

80% of those questioned had more than one online profile. The majority of participants used at least 2 methods of online promotion, with some using up to 6. After a website or blog, the most popular additional profiles were Facebook and Twitter. The only social network which none of the respondents used was Flickr. This is a site which allows users to share images and communicate with other artists and potential clients, however it is possibly more suited to photographers than illustrators.

The option was given for respondents to include methods not listed, in the form of the *Other(please specify)* response. 10% of respondents gave an answer for the 'Other' option. One response given for this category was Behance. This is a site which provides online portfolios for professionals, in the guise of a social networking site. Among other things, this allows potential employers to search for suitable creative talent. Pinterest (2013), an image sharing site, was also listed as a site used for self-promotion by one respondent.

The second part of section two asked respondents whether they were worried about the effect of the Internet on their professional reputation. 65% of respondents answered yes to this question. This is a majority, albeit a small one, which suggests that the use of online promotional methods does lead people in this group to worry about their professional reputation and how it is affected by the use of the internet as a promotional tool. The percentage answering that they were worried about the potential risks was lower than expected. However, this could be for a number of reasons which should become clearer through analysis of the subsequent questions. It is possible that respondents do not feel worried because they are not aware of the risks which the internet poses to them or, alternatively, they are not worried because although they identify that there are risks, they are in a position where they feel they are able to comfortably mitigate these risks and prevent any serious problems from occurring.

4.3   Section three: Perceptions of risk.

Section three was split into two main questions, both consisting of grid array style answer schemes and requiring the respondent to rate a number of scenarios or possible outcomes on a scale from 1 to 5.

The first question in section three asked participants to rate a number of possible actions or scenarios in order to determine how much of a risk they think they pose. The scenarios were rated from 1 to 5, with 5 being a high risk, to show how much of a risk participants considered they posed to their professional reputation. All of the given scenarios received an average rating of between 2 and 4. This illustrates that there wasn't one clear issue as there was a wide range of different responses for each scenario listed. Responses of 3 suggest that participants are neither worried about nor confident in a scenario, and instead are somewhat neutral. Along the same lines, ratings of 2 or 4 suggest a tendency towards worry or comfort but no strong view either way. It is therefore important to consider not just the average marks received but also the numbers of extreme responses of 1 or 5. This is because responses of 1 or 5 suggest that a respondent is definitely not worried at all about a scenario, or is definitely worried that it could be a problem respectively.

The scenario which was consistently given the highest rating was "*Images others post of you on social media*". The average mark assigned to this scenario was 3.61. Female respondents rated this scenario higher, with an average rating of 4, whereas male respondents gave an average rating of just 3.42. Interestingly, respondents in their second year of study gave this scenario a much lower rating than those in their third year. The average rating from the second years was just 2.5 compared to an average of 3.85 from third year students.

However, scenario 2 "*Comments/ text posted by others on your website*" actually received the highest number of '5' ratings, suggesting that it was at the extreme of being something which respondents definitely worry about. This scenario received an average rating of 3.44, with ratings of 3.25 and 3.83 from males and females respectively. Again, for this scenario ratings were much lower from second year students, with the average being just 2.75 compared to an average of 3.54 from third year students. Scenario 3, "*Images/ video you post on your website*" was not seen as much of a risk and was given an average rating of just 2.56, where 5 was taken to be the highest possible level of risk. This scenario also received the highest number of ratings of 1, supporting the idea that a lot of respondents were not overly worried about this scenario. Here, female respondents again gave a higher average rating, this time of 2.83, with males giving an average mark of 2.42 out of 5. Second and third year responses were very similar here, with averages of 2.25 and 2.46 respectively. For eight out of the ten scenarios, female respondents gave a higher average risk rating than male respondents, which suggests an overall higher level of perceived risk.

For the first 6 scenarios, the options which involve materials posted by the users themselves received consistently lower ratings than those which looked at materials posted by others. This illustrates the idea that people feel much more in control of what they post themselves and feel that they are a lot less likely to damage their reputation themselves. Scenarios 2, 4 and 6 received average ratings of between 3 and 4, whereas scenarios 1, 3 and 5 averaged ratings between 2 and 3. The idea of monitoring what others say and post about you is a very important one and central to staying safe and correctly represented online. Therefore it is a very good result to see that the majority of those questioned are already aware of the risks associated with this. It will be important to emphasize this in the materials, and to discuss any possible steps which can be taken to lower the level of risk and make respondents feel safer and less worried about what others may put on the internet about them and how it will affect their reputation. Figure 1: *Scenarios and their average risk ratings* shows each risk along with its average risk rating.

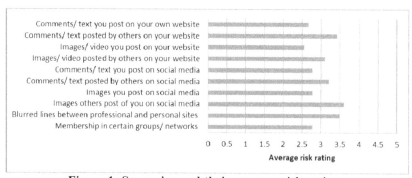

Figure 1: Scenarios and their average risk ratings

This question also gave the option to suggest any scenarios which had not been mentioned. There were two suggestions, both of which related to having work stolen. As one participant put it: *"People stealing my work. I never put proper work on my blog or twitter, only my website. i take pictures of the screen so it is harder for someone to take what is mine"* (Participant 4)

This idea of work being stolen and perhaps used inappropriately or without proper permission had not previously been considered. This is an issue that also appeared in the next question.

The second part of section three considered the possible negative effects that could occur as a result of online promotion. Participants were again asked to rate a number of statements from 1 to 5, this time based on how worried they were about them happening. The effect which respondents were most worried about was *"Negative impact on employment"*, which received an average rating of 3.44 and a rating of 5 out of 5 from 22% of those questioned. This was the highest number of 5 ratings of any of the options. The average ratings from male and female respondents were very similar, with males giving marginally higher ratings with an average of 3.5 and females averaging a rating of 3.33 out of 5. Second year students gave this effect an average rating of 3, whereas third years gave a slightly higher average of 3.54.

Respondents were much less worried about *"Negative effect on image/ reputation"* or *"Potential employers searching for your information"*, as both of these received average ratings of just 2.94 and 2.89 respectively. For the scenario *"Potential employers searching for your information"* 28% of respondents gave a rating of only 1, showing no worry at all related to this risk. While second and third years did not differ greatly on their average marks for this particular scenario, they differed quite significantly when rating the *"Negative effect on image/ reputation"*. While third years gave an average rating of 2.77, respondents in their second year of study gave a higher average rating of 3.55. Figure 2 shows the possible effects and their average rating.

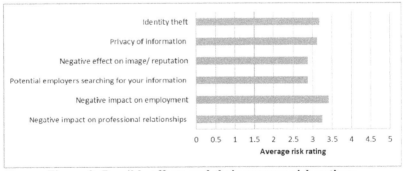

Figure 2: Possible effects and their average risk ratings.

This shows that four out of the six risks listed were given ratings of 3 or above by the majority of participants. It can therefore be assumed that these negative effects do provide a considerable source of worry/ stress to those questioned. In fact, when considering male and female averages separately, male respondents gave every possible effect a risk rating of 3 or above, whereas female respondent only gave 4 out of the 6 a rating over 3.

Again, this question gave the opportunity to suggest effects which the researcher had not considered. In this case there was only one response, which was very much unexpected: *"My web presence may affect my ability to join a service or military position"* (Participant 15). While this is an interesting effect and not one which had previously been considered, it is not necessarily something which can be dealt with or referenced in the support document, as it applies to a specific situation and is unlikely to be relevant to the majority of the target audience.

4.4   Section four: Personal experience of risk.

Section four asked participants if they had ever personally experienced any of the negative effects of having a professional presence online. While the majority of participants answered no to this question, one respondent said yes. Those who answered yes were asked to give details of their experiences. One third year male student respondent had experienced work being stolen. He gave details of having work put on a site and entered into a competition by someone else: *"I had an image of mine used for a competition on Threadless.com. luckily I spotted it before it was too late but it was on its way to winning"* (Participant 13). This negative experience and the concept of protecting personal work was mentioned by a number of participants in the previous section of questions as well. This was not previously taken into account as a risk, but following this research it was seen as an important element to include within the support materials.

Protecting work online is a difficult task. Work is covered by copyright law as soon as it is created, however this is very difficult and costly to actually enforce. Methods of protecting personal property and the effect which this has on professional reputation were therefore considered in order to include this within the support materials.

4.5   Section five: Mitigation steps.

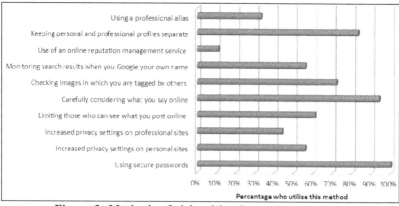

Figure 3: Methods of risk mitigation and percentage of respondents who use them.

Section five asked participants what methods they employed in order to mitigate any possible risks and protect their online reputation. They were asked to choose all that applied from a given list. All of the participants employed at least one of the methods listed, with many employing multiple safeguards and some employing up to 9 of them. The most common method employed was using secure passwords, which was used by 100% of those questioned. Figure 3 shows the different methods suggested and the percentage of respondents who use them.

94% of respondents said that they carefully consider what they post online, and 83% protect their reputation and identity online by keeping personal and professional profiles separate. Both of these methods of mitigation were used by 100% of female respondents. Male respondent numbers were slightly lower, with 92% carefully considering what they post online and 75% keeping personal and professional profiles separate.

56% of respondents said that they monitor the search results obtained by Googling their own name, and 33% said they use a professional alias to further keep personal and professional profiles separate. The latter figure was the same for both male and female respondents. However, the number using a professional alias was considerably higher for third year students. While 38% of third year respondents said they use this mitigation step, none of the second years questioned currently do this. This will therefore be considered in the support document.

Interestingly, 11% of those questioned said that they used online reputation management tools to protect their professional reputation. One of these respondents was a lecturer and therefore more established as a professional illustrator. The other was a female third year illustration student. While it is possibly more likely for professional illustrators and those established in the field, it was unexpected to find any students using these services. This is an area which is important to mention in the support materials, as free tools are available which can be very useful.

Other than those options listed, only one participant suggested any other alternative methods of protecting identity or professional reputation. This method concerned uploading low quality images in order to protect intellectual property and hence protect professional reputation in the process. This was not an area considered previously, but it was also mentioned in responses to section 3 of the questionnaire. This was therefore taken into consideration during the design of supporting materials.

5   Conclusions and the future

From this study, it was possible to determine the main areas in which guidance was needed and to create a PDF document intended to support those with an online presence and help them to monitor and protect their online reputation. The full support document can be seen in Figure 4.

Taking charge of your online reputation

If you are going to use the Internet to promote your work and yourself as an artist, there are a number of important points to consider:

- ☐ Monitor and Moderate what you post and others post about you online
- ☐ Remember, it's permanent.
- ☐ Keep your private life private
- ☐ Protect your work
- ☐ Google yourself!
- ☐ Consider the use of reputation management tools.

A study by Microsoft found that **47% of UK employers use publicly available online information when examining potential job candidates** and **41%** have rejected candidates based on their online reputation.

Firstly, the basics: Monitor and Moderate

- ✓ **Set high security levels** on social networks so that people only see what you want them to see.
- ✓ **Monitor what others post about you** on these sites, checking to see whenever you are tagged in something – it's harder to control what others say and do so try and keep on top of this and remove anything you don't want there as quickly as possible.
- ✓ **Moderate comments on websites or blogs.** This takes a little extra time, but means you are fully in control of what goes up on your own site.

Permanency

- ✓ Remember, once something's on the internet, it can be very hard to get rid of, so **always think before you post!**
- ✓ **Post positively** and think about the repercussions. Studies have shown that the greatest reason for rejecting a potential job candidate is *"inappropriate comments or text written by the candidate"*

Keep your private life private

- ✓ Maintain **separate email accounts** for work and pleasure.
- ✓ Maintain **separate social networking accounts.**
- ✓ Keep **high security settings on personal accounts** (the second highest reason for rejecting a candidate in the Microsoft study was *"unsuitable photos or videos"*, so this step helps to keep potential employers away from the photos of you in a tiger onesie when you'd had one too many)

Protect your work.

- ✓ **Use low resolution images** on websites and blogs to lower the chance of plagiarism.
- ✓ Look into **digital watermarking** – costly, but could be worth it. Images can be tracked around the world and are always associated to you by a watermark embedded within the code of the image itself. More information available at Digimarc.com.

Google yourself.

- ✓ **Monitor what comes up on the first page** of a Google search for your own name.
- ✓ **Set up Google Alerts** to keep on top of what people are searching for along with your name.
- ✓ **Claim your namespace on all the social networks** – when people search for you, social networks are favored by Google, so try to fill your 'first page' with these.

Reputation management.

- ✓ Companies such as BrandYourself.com offer free tools to help manage professional reputation. Particularly useful if there's something negative you wish would go away.

Further Reading

- ✓ The Microsoft study mentioned above
- ✓ UK Safer Internet Centre resources
- ✓ Facebook Checklist

Designed by Rebecca Brett 2013 ©

Figure 4: Taking charge of your online reputation - support document.

Through exploring the use of social networking and other online methods employed by a number of illustration students, it was possible to determine what steps they were taking to mitigate the risks to their professional reputation. By determining the main areas which worried these participants it was then possible to produce support materials to help them overcome these issues and mitigate the risks. These materials were tested by the target audience and the prototype was improved so that it met their needs as closely as possible. These materials will be made available to the participants of the study as well as other self-employed individuals if they require them.

The document created focuses on the main points where it was determined that further education could be helpful. These areas were predominantly relating to emphasising the permanency of anything posted on the internet and hence the idea that it is important to think carefully before posting anything. Points were made about keeping personal and private profiles as separate as possible and protecting work using low resolution images or digital watermarking. Subsequently, it was suggested that users regularly Google their own name to monitor any changes in the results and furthermore consider the use of a reputation management tool and other pre-existing support materials.

Further study would definitely be useful in this area, as it is important to investigate the perceptions of professionals and ensure that materials are available to help them protect their online identity and reputation. Further research could consider a larger sample from the same group in order to gain more knowledge of the views of those using the internet for self-promotion. Alternatively, investigation could involve other professions, in order to create targeted materials and compare the views of those in different professions. For example, research is continually being carried out on behalf of Microsoft for their annual Data Privacy Day. This covers a different area of online safety each year, for example in 2013 this involved study of "consumers' perceptions about how their information is used online". (DataPrivacyDay, 2013)

6   References

Bachelor L (2013). *Self-employed worker numbers soar in UK*. (Online) Available at: http://www.guardian.co.uk/money/2013/feb/06/self-employed-worker-numbers-soar-uk [Accessed April 2013]

DataPrivacyDay (2013). *Consumers Need More Help Controlling their Personal Information Online.* (Online) Available at: http://www.microsoft.com/security/online-privacy/overview.aspx [Accessed August 2013]

GOFS, (2012). *Future Identities: Changing identities in the UK: the next 10 years.* (Online) Available at: http://www.bis.gov.uk/foresight/our-work/policy-futures/identity [Accessed February 2013]

Griffiths, M. (2012). *Childrens' Excessive Social Networking: A Brief Overview of the Empirical Literature.* (Online) Available at: http://www.saferinternet.org.uk/downloads/ Research_Highlights/UKCCIS_RH_30_Excessive_social_networking.pdf [Accessed February 2013]

Kuss, D & Griffiths, M. (2011). Online social networking and addiction - a review of the psychological literature. *International journal of environmental research and public health*. 8. pp3528-3552.

LSE. (2013). *EU Kids Online*. Online. Available at: http://www2.lse.ac.uk/media@lse/research/EUKidsOnline/Home.aspx [Accessed February 2013]

NASUWT, (2012). *Pupils using social media to bully teachers*. (Online) Available at: http://www.nasuwt.org.uk/Whatsnew/NASUWTNews/PressReleases/PupilsUsingSocialMedia ToBullyTeachers [Accessed February 2013]

O'Neill, B., Livingstone, S. and McLaughlin, S. (2011). *Final recommendations for policy, methodology and research*. LSE, London: EU Kids Online. (Online) Available at: http://www2.lse.ac.uk/media@lse/research/EUKidsOnline/D7.pdf [Accessed February 2013]

Phippen, A. (2011). *The Online Abuse of Professionals*. Research Report from the UK Safer Internet Centre. (Online) Available at: http://www.swgfl.org.uk/staying-safe/files/documents/prof-abuse-full-report [Accessed February 2013]

Shariff, S. (2008). *Cyber Bullying: Issues and solutions for the school, the classroom and the home*. Abingdon: Routledge.

Smith, C (2013). *How Many People Use the Top Social Media, Apps & Services?* (Online) Available at: http://expandedramblings.com/index.php/resource-how-many-people-use-the-top-social-media/ [Accessed August 2013]

Stauffer, S., Heath, M. A., Coyne, S. M. & Ferrin, S. (2012), High school teachers' perceptions of cyberbullying prevention and intervention strategies. *Psychology in the Schools*. 49:4 pp352-367.

UKSIC (2013). *UK Safer Internet Centre: Professional Reputation* (Online) Available at: http://www.saferinternet.org.uk/advice-and-resources/teachers-and-professionals/professional-reputation [Accessed February 2013]

New Method for Numerical Approximations of Vector Derivatives Based on Digital Signal Processing Techniques

H.Brice and M.Z.Ahmed

Center for Security, Communications and Network Research,
Plymouth University, Plymouth, United Kingdom
e-mail: info@cscan.org

Abstract

Accurate propagation models are required for predicting the propagation of electromagnetic waves within complex environments. This paper proposes the use of a new method to accurately compute the divergence and curl of electromagnetic fields. The computation of the derivatives of vector fields is normally approximated using numerical methods such as the Finite-Difference Time-Domain Method (FDTD), the Finite Integration Technique and the Multi-Resolution Time-Domain Method. These methods are all limited in terms of their accuracy, resolution, computational efficiency and numerical stability. This paper introduces a new method for computing derivatives based on Two-Dimensional (2D) Digital Signal Processing (DSP) techniques. The method involves computing a numerical approximation of the derivative of a function by considering the frequency domain definition of the derivative and designing a 2D finite impulse response (FIR) filter that implements the differentiation. Appropriate windowing functions are used to ensure that the FIR response is as close to the ideal 2D differentiator response as possible. This paper provides an example where the curl of a vector field is determined using this method and accuracy within a few percent is achieved. The proposed innovative method can be extended to three dimensions and used to find numerical solutions of Maxwell's Equations, thus allowing it to be applied to the design of accurate propagation models.

1   Introduction

The effective design of wireless communications systems requires realistic models that describe the electromagnetic propagation within the environment in which the system is intended to be used. There are various numerical methods that are used to model electromagnetic propagation by providing numerical solutions to Maxwell's Equations. These include the Finite-Difference Time-Domain Method (Yee, 1966), the Finite Integration Technique (Weiland, 1977) and the Multi-Resolution Time-Domain method (Krumpholz and Katehi, 1996).

Numerous limitations with current methods have been examined. These include issues of accuracy (Shlager and Schneider, 2003), computational efficiency (Aoyagi and Jin-Fa Lee amd Mittra, 1993) and numerical stability (Thoma and Weiland, 1998).

Various improvements to existing methods have been suggested to overcome these limitations (Wu and Itoh, 1997). Recent research has attempted to minimise problems such as numerical dispersion within the Finite-Difference Time-Domain method (Finkelstein and Kastner, 2007). There has also been interest in the development of new algorithms based on existing methods (Cole, 2002), hardware implementation of these methods (Junkin, 2011) and also in the application of propagation methods to complex structures, such as buildings (Mock, 2011).

This paper proposes a new method that can be used for electromagnetic propagation modelling based on multi-dimensional Digital Signal Processing (DSP).

The design of a two-dimensional (2D) Finite Impulse Response (FIR) Differentiator is presented followed by a discussion concerning the application of 2D window functions that are used to improve the filter's response. The filter is then tested by applying it to the computation of the curl of a known vector field in two dimensions, thus showing that this method can be used for the modelling of electromagnetic propagation.

2   Design Methodology

The design process was conducted with the aim of demonstrating the use of DSP in solving known problems relating to vector fields and thus establishing that DSP methods can be used within propagation models by finding numerical solutions to Maxwell's Equations. Throughout the design process numerical results were compared and contrasted with empirical results in order to establish that accurate numerical results were obtained.

The process began by considering the standard Finite Impulse Response (FIR) differentiator followed by the corresponding 2D version. The extension of one-dimensional Window Functions into two dimensions was also considered and the effect of these functions on the 2D frequency response of the filter was investigated. The filter was tested by using it to find the curl of known vector functions.

3   Finite Impulse Response Differentiators

A differentiator in the frequency domain is known to have a linear magnitude response and a pi/2 phase offset. The angular frequency response is given by

$$H(\theta) = \theta e^{i(0.5\pi - 0.5\pi N)}$$

Where θ is the angular frequency and N is the number of coefficients. Note that the number of coefficients for an FIR Differentiator must be odd and the impulse response is given by

$$h(n) = \frac{i}{2\pi} \int_{-\pi}^{\pi} \theta e^{i\theta(n - 0.5N)} d\theta$$

Where n = 1, 2 ...N - 1, and h(0) = 0. FIR differentiators can also be considered in two dimensions (Tseng, 2003).

$$H_{2D}(\theta, \phi) = (i\theta)(i\phi)e^{-i(\theta+\phi)}$$

In this equation, θ refers to the angular frequency in the x direction and ϕ to the angular frequency in the y direction. Throughout this paper the size of the 2D FIR filter (N * M) is defined by setting N = 11 and M = 11.

4   Use of Window Functions

Window functions, which are used in one-dimensional DSP to overcome issues related to the truncation of the filter coefficients, can also be extended into two dimensions. Consider a typical one-dimensional Kaiser Window whose coefficients are given by

$$k(n) = \frac{I_0\left(10\sqrt{1 - \left(\frac{2n}{N-1}\right)^2}\right)}{I_0(10)}$$

In the above expression, I0 is the zeroth order Modified Bessel Function of the first kind. The 2D version (Fig. 1) of this Kaiser Window can then be found.

$$k_{2D}(n, m) = k\left(\sqrt{(m-5)^2 + (n-5)^2}\right)$$

The frequency response of an ideal differentiator is given in Fig. 2, and the designed differentiator is given in Fig. 4. The response given in Fig. 3 shows the differentiator without the 2D Kaiser Window.

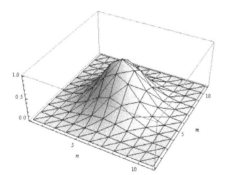
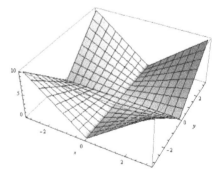

Figure 1: Ideal Differentiator Response

Figure 2: Ideal Differentiator Response

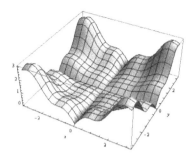 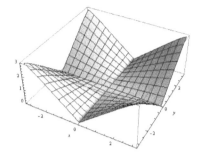

Figure 3: 2D Truncated FIR Impulse Response   **Figure 4: 2D Windowed FIR Impulse Response**

5   Computing the Curl of a Vector Field

A 2D vector field can be represented as follows:

$$\vec{F} = F_x\mathbf{x} + F_y\mathbf{\hat{y}}$$

Where ^x and ^y are the unit vectors and Fx and Fy are the respective projections. The curl can be defined as follows.

$$\nabla \times \vec{F} = \left(\frac{\partial F_y}{\partial x} - \frac{\partial F_x}{\partial y}\right)\mathbf{\hat{z}}$$

Two matrices are considered, Fx and Fy, which contain the values of a vector function at discrete, equally spaced values indicating the projections along the x and y axes respectively. The matrices Dx and Dy represent approximations of the partial derivatives of the x components with respect to y and the y components with respect to x respectively. Let X represent the matrix of FIR coefficients of size N * M.

$$D_y = F_y * X$$

$$D_x^T = F_x^T * X$$

From these matrices it is possible to compute the curl.

$$curl \approx D_y - D_x$$

For example an input vector function (Fig. 5) is selected and the curl obtained using the FIR filter (Fig. 7). This can be compared with the empirical result (Fig. 6) and a finite difference time domain differentiation (Fig. 8) to demonstrate the effectiveness of the FIR filter.

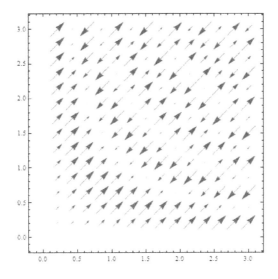

Figure 5: Input Vector Function

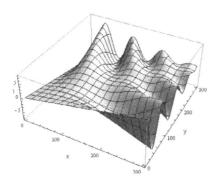

Figure 6: Ideal Curl   **Figure 7: 2D Windowed FIR Curl**

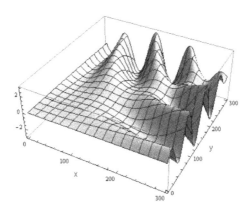

Figure 8: FDTD Curl

6   Conclusion

This paper shows that the proposed method can be used as a basis for designing accurate propagation models by computing numerical solutions of Maxwell's Equations. The comparisons show that it can provide a significant improvement over the Finite-Difference Time-Domain method. The scaling effect introduced in the windowing stage applies equally across the filter and can be corrected using a scaling factor. It can be seen that the application of the window function leads to a differentiator design that is much closer to the ideal than what can be achieved by using a non-windowed filter with the same number of filter coefficients.

7   Suggestions for Further Research

It is possible to extend the filter to three dimensions, which would be advantageous when considering complex environments such as buildings. The design of a three-dimensional filter with the investigation of its applications within propagation models can form the basis of future research. It is also important to carry out further investigations into the comparisons between this proposed method and ones that are currently in use. Furthermore, the scope of this method and its applications to areas other than those mentioned here is an area for further investigation as numerical methods are used extensively throughout engineering and scientific research.

8   Acknowledgments

The authors would like to thank Matthew Taylor and Lee Davis for their support and the IET, SPIE and the School of Computing and Mathematics at the University of Plymouth for financial contributions.

9   References

Aoyagi, P. and Jin-Fa Lee and Mittra, R. (1993). A hybrid yee algorithm/scalar-wave equation approach. IEEE Transactions on Microwave Theory and Techniques, 41(9): 1593-1600.

Cole, J. B. (2002). High-accuracy yee algorithm based on nonstandard finite differences: New developments and verifications. IEEE Trans. Antennas Propag., 50(9): 1185-1191.

Finkelstein, B. and Kastner, R. (2007). Finite difference time domain dispersion reduction schemes. J. Comput. Phys., 221(1): 422-438.

Junkin, G. (2011). Conformal fdtd modeling of imperfect conductors at millimeter wave bands. IEEE Transactions on Antennas and Propagation, 59(1): 199-205.

Krumpholz, M. and Katehi, L. (1996). MRTD: new time-domain schemes based on multiresolution analysis. IEEE Transactions on Microwave Theory and Techniques, 44(4): 555-571.

Mock, A. (2011). Compact fdtd formulation for structures with spherical invariance. IEEE Transactions on Antennas and Propagation, 59(3): 987-993.

Shlager, K. L. and Schneider, J. B. (2003). Comparison of the dispersion properties of several low-dispersion finite difference time-domain algorithms. IEEE Transactions on Antennas and Propagation., 51(3): 642-653.

Thoma, P. and Weiland, T. (1998). Numerical stability of finite difference time domain methods. IEEE Transactions on Magnetics, 34(5): 1302-1309.

Tseng, C.-C. (2003). Design of 2-D variable fractional delay FIR filter using 2-D differentiators. International Symposium on Circuits and Systems, 4: 189-192.

Weiland, T. (1977). A discretization model for the solution of maxwell's equations for six-component fields. Archiv fuer Elektronik und Uebertragungstechnik, 31: 116-120.

Wu, R.-B. and Itoh, T. (1997). Hybrid finite-difference time-domain modeling of curved surfaces using tetrahedral edge elements. IEEE Transactions on Antennas and Propagation, 45(8): 1302-1309.

Yee, K. (1966). Numerical solution of initial boundary value problems involving maxwell's equations in isotropic media. IEE Transactions on Antennas and Propagation, 14(3): 302-307.
9

Automatic Vision-based Disease Detection in Blood Samples by a Medical Robot

O.Clark and G.Bugmann

School of Computing and Mathematics, Plymouth University, Plymouth, UK
e-mail: guido.bugmann@plymouth.ac.uk

Abstract

Manual diagnosis of Malaria and Chagas disease via light microscopy can be time consuming and requires a trained microscopist, which can be a problem in many of the areas where these diseases are most prevalent. In this paper a solution to automate the detection of the Plasmodium vivax and Trypanosoma cruzi parasites has been developed by adapting a conventional manually operated microscope for control via a computer. An application was developed to control the microscope to obtain focused images of a sample, the sample is then checked for the presence of the parasites. Results for the microscope control, focusing, artefact removal and segmentation of the images were good. However disease classification results produced by two support vector machines were poor.

Keywords

Robot, Microscope, Malaria, Chagas Disease, Automated Focus

1   Introduction

Parasitic diseases are a major problem for many poorer countries. In 2010 there were an estimated 216 million Malaria infections caused by the parasite species Plasmodium, approximately 81% of which occurred in the African region. Out of those infected there were an estimated 655,000 deaths due to the disease (World Health Organization, 2011). Another parasitic disease is Chagas caused by the Trypanosoma cruzi parasite. The Chagas disease is most common in South America with an estimated 7 to 8 million infections worldwide (World Health Organization, 2013).

Diagnosis of these diseases can be achieved through the use of light microscopy, however in countries that either have high or low rates of infection the accuracy of the diagnosis can be poor, due primarily to there being too few trained microscopists who are required to analyse a large number of samples. Also in areas where the diseases are not common, infections may be missed due to a lack of familiarity with detecting the diseases (Milne et al. 1994).

The aim of this project is to produce a robotic microscope that takes a slide with a stained thin film blood smear, obtains automatically focused images from the slide which are then analysed to determine whether the Trypanosoma cruzi or Plasmodium vivax parasites are present.

2   Background

Various methods have been attempted to automate the detection of the parasites which cause Malaria through the use of automated vision systems.

In (Savkare and Narote, 2011) a technique is demonstrated for the extraction and separation of red blood cells from an image, as well as the use of an SVM classifier for the detection of Malaria which used geometric, colour and statistical based features. This system was shown to perform reliably on a set of 15 samples.

Unlike the problem of detecting the parasites which cause Malaria, there is relatively little research on the detection of Chagas disease through the use of automated vision systems. One of the few pieces of research into the automation of light microscopy for analysing thin film blood smears to detect the presence of Trypanosoma cruzi is (Uc-Cetina et al. 2013) where feature extraction was used on the black spot which is the parasite's DNA before classification through the use of Gaussian discriminant analysis. The resulting classification gave a true negative rate of 0.8437 and a true positive rate of 0.9833 showing that this technique worked well on their samples. However on the sample used for this project no DNA spot is visible in the Trypanosoma cruzi parasites.

In (Maitra et al. 2012) the Hough circle transform (Yuen et al. 1990) is used for the detection and counting of red blood cells, although this paper is not focused on Malaria or Chagas a technique is demonstrated which can be used to detect the locations of blood cells from a slide containing a thin blood smear.

Adapting a standard manually operated microscope has been attempted before, one successful example can be seen in (Barber, 2005). The main reason for developing your own system rather than buying a pre-built automated microscope is that often the manufacturers design them with only set tasks in mind. The result is that the modifications are expensive and time consuming, especially with regards to the software side.

2.1   Previous Work

Previously two aspects of the project had been worked on prior to this project, firstly the hardware needed to move the slide containing the sample across the microscope's stage, and secondly software to detect the presence of the Trypanosoma cruzi and Plasmodium vivax parasites.

The implementation of the slide mover mechanics involving the mounting of two stepper motors and the gearing to connect them to the slide mover controls was completed; as well as a prototype of the electronics needed to control the stepper motors. The details of this work can be seen in (Perocheau, 2012). The result was a partial success, however due to the use of a 1:1 gear ratio the stepper motors were unable to move the slide mover; these gears were later replaced by gears with a ratio of 12:5, which allowed the stepper motors to move the slide mover.

The second aspect of the project worked on previously was the software used to detect the presence of the Trypanosoma cruzi and Plasmodium vivax parasites, with a focus on extracting features to classify a sample as to whether it is infected with one of the two parasites or is not infected (Katsadoraki, 2012). However the results were poor with both the parasite and red blood cell detection producing poor results.

3   Methodology

There are two distinct areas to this project, the hardware and the software.

3.1   Microscope Hardware

The microscope used for this project is a standard manually operated Vickers optical microscope. Initially automation was only implemented in the slide mover, which moves the sample slide around the microscope's stage. To improve on this a third stepper motor connected via a chain and two sprockets automated focusing of the microscope. The chain and sprockets drive was chosen over other methods of connecting the stepper motor to the microscope due to the lateral movement of the microscope's control, which can be seen in Figure 1. A gear ratio of 3:1 was chosen to reduce the amount of torque required to turn the microscope's fine focus adjustment knob by the stepper motor, the low gear ratio also improves the accuracy and allows for finer control. Additionally four snap action switches were added to detect when the maximum or minimum positions of the slide mover are reached.

Figure 1: The composited image shows the 6mm of lateral movement in the microscope's control which necessitated the use of the chain drive.

Figure 2: The completed microscope hardware

On the electronics side the system was rewired and placed into a box. As the original stepper motor control electronics was designed to only control two stepper motors, this was extended with the possibility of controlling up to four motors as well as the ability to receive inputs from up to six analogue or digital sensors.

The system primarily consists of an Arduino Uno and four stepper motor controllers in an enclosure. The completed microscope hardware and control box can be seen in Figure 2 on the previous page.

3.2   Software for Focusing On, Enhancing and Detecting Parasites

The software developed for this project is split into three different parts, the first part of the software is used to control the physical movements of the microscope and consists of embedded code running on the Arduino Uno and a Python based program that communicates with the Arduino Uno over a virtual serial port and microscope camera, both connected via USB.

The second part of the software is used to obtain focused images from the microscope and to remove artefacts and uneven lighting. This is achieved by moving the slide on the stage in the x and y axis through the use of the slide mover stepper motors. Once the desired location to take the sample has been reached, a set of fifty images are taken at different focus levels. These images contain uneven lighting and artefacts, caused by the microscope's illumination system, optics and contaminants on the optics. This is reduced or removed through the use of a priori image which is obtained before a slide is loaded. The sample images are corrected using the acquisition based division technique (Likar and Pernus, 2000), where each colour value for each pixel on the sample image is divided by the corresponding pixels' colour values from the priori image, before being multiplied by a constant to restore the colour. This process can be seen in Figure 3.

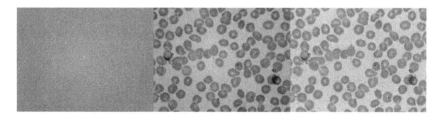

Figure 3: On the left is the priori image taken when no slide is loaded, in the middle is a sample before correction, on the right is the sample after correction.

Once each of the set of fifty images has been corrected, Hough circle transform is used to detect the presence of circles which in this case is the red blood cells. As the sample comes into focus the number of circles detected peaks. The results are smoothed by taking the mean of the sample and the closest four results, to attempt to produce a single peak value. The original image corresponding to the peak value which is considered as the best focused is then stored for analysis.

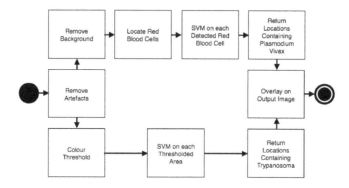

Figure 4: Algorithm steps used to detect the presence of Plasmodium vivax or Trypanosoma cruzi in an image.

In the third software step the best focused samples are analysed to attempt to detect the presence of Trypanosoma cruzi or Plasmodium vivax. An overview of the algorithm used to perform this task can be seen in Figure 4.

Two different techniques are used to detect Trypanosoma cruzi and Plasmodium vivax, both are based on the use of support vector machines set up to classify on histograms of the located red blood cells, and potential areas that may contain a Trypanosoma cruzi parasite (Chapelle et al. 1999).

The two support vector machines are manually trained by showing sections of sample images to an operator that contain either a red blood cell which may or may not be infected with the Plasmodium vivax parasite, or a location that potentially contains a Trypanosoma cruzi parasite. The operator classifies these areas until the required number of training examples is achieved. Once the required number is reached the two support vector machines are trained using the examples.

4   Results

To produce the results a set of 100 samples were taken from the three available slides, 25 from the Plasmodium vivax good slide, 25 from the Plasmodium vivax faulty slide and 50 from the Trypanosoma cruzi slide so as to balance each type of parasite to be detected. The sample locations were selected by hand and chosen to include both areas where the sample is well spread and stained as well as areas where the blood cells are not spread well, are damaged or poor staining has occurred during the slide's preparation.

4.1   Focus Measure

The results for the automation of focusing the microscope can be seen in Figure 5, where the difference in steps between the automated best focused image is compared to the best manually chosen focused image. The optimal focus of 66% of the samples was found by the automated system, and 96% of the samples were within 8 steps of the optimal focus, which provides a good enough image for analysis to be performed.

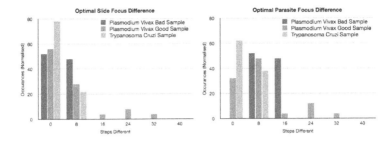

Figure 5: On the left is the difference in steps between the human and computer selected best focus levels for each slide, on the right is the difference in steps between the human and computer selected best focus for viewing the parasites.

However the focal position that is optimal for viewing the red blood cells is not always optimal for viewing the parasites, this can be seen in the second chart in Figure 5, where for the Plasmodium vivax bad sample 52% of the optimal viewing focus level was 8 steps out with the remaining 48% being 16 steps from optimal.

4.2 Plasmodium Vivax Detection and Classification

As discussed in the methodology the Plasmodium vivax classification is achieved through two stages. The first stage corrects any uneven brightness, reduces artefacts and detects the location of the red blood cells.

Slide	Located Red Blood Cells	Missed Red Blood Cells	Percentage Missed
Plasmodium Vivax Sample One (Faulty)	2269	602	20.97
Plasmodium Vivax Sample Two (Good)	2380	1028	30.16
Trypanosoma Cruzi Sample	6734	578	7.90
Combined Results	11383	2208	16.25

Slide	Average True Positives	Average False Positives	Average True Negatives	Average False Negatives
Plasmodium Vivax Sample One (Faulty)	1.68	7.52	60.48	21.08
Plasmodium Vivax Sample Two (Good)	6.92	18.04	42.6	27.64
Trypanosoma Cruzi Sample	0	5.28	129.4	0
Combined Results	2.15	9.03	90.47	12.18

Table 1: Showing the results for red blood cell detection in the first table and the Plasmodium vivax classification results in the second table.

In Table 1, left table, the percentage of red blood cells missed between slides can be seen to vary a great deal, with the performance of both of the Plasmodium vivax slides being considerably worse than that of the Trypanosoma cruzi slide. This is primarily down to the Plasmodium vivax slides having a higher rate of poor spreading and damaged red blood cells, caused during the preparation of the slides.

The second stage takes the red blood cells that have been detected and attempts to classify them as either containing the Plasmodium vivax parasite or not containing the Plasmodium vivax parasite. The results shown in the right table in Table 1 from this stage are poor with a tendency to over classify as not containing the Plasmodium vivax parasite, with the true positive classification being low across both infected slides.

4.3 Trypanosoma Cruzi Detection and Classification

Slide	Average True Positives	Average False Positives	Average False Negatives
Plasmodium Vivax Sample One (Faulty)	0	2.04	0
Plasmodium Vivax Sample Two (Good)	0	8.52	0
Trypanosoma Cruzi Sample	2.48	0.24	0.86
Combined Results	1.24	2.76	0.43

Slide	Average True Positives	Average False Positives	Average True Negatives	Average False Negatives
Plasmodium Vivax Sample One (Faulty)	0	0.44	4.92	0
Plasmodium Vivax Sample Two (Good)	0	2.16	17.2	0
Trypanosoma Cruzi Sample	0.84	0.32	0.28	2.5
Combined Results	0.42	0.81	5.67	1.25

Table 2: Table showing the results for red blood cell detection in the first table and the Trypanosoma cruzi classification results in the second table.

As with the plasmodium vivax detection and classification the Trypanosoma cruzi detection and classification is split into two stages. The first stage uses colour thresholding to detect areas in an image that potentially contain Trypanosoma cruzi.

In Table 2 the results shown in the left table from the colour thresholding are promising where the number of areas selected attempts to minimise the number of false negatives as these are to be corrected in the second stage. Thus the goal is to locate all Trypanosoma cruzi even if this means selecting some areas which do not contain any. The average number of Trypanosoma cruzi in an image taken from the Trypanosoma cruzi slide is 3.34 which is quite close to the number of true positives for that slide at 2.48. True negatives are not counted at this stage as this encompasses all other parts of the image where an object is not detected or an undetected Trypanosoma cruzi is located.

The second stage results as with the Plasmodium vivax classifier is poor, with a trend towards classifying detected areas as not containing a parasite when there is one present giving an increase to the rate of false negatives.

5 Conclusion

The final results regarding the classification of the two parasites was poor, however the other aspects of the project including the hardware, focusing, lighting correction, background removal, red blood cell detection and potential Trypanosoma cruzi detection worked well. In particular the microscope hardware and the software controlling the hardware worked well allowing the sample collection using the automated focusing software to obtain images that were on average at or close to being in focus.

Overall the system needs further development and testing in several areas before it can be used to perform accurate and quick diagnosis of blood samples. Additional slides are needed for testing and verifying the system before an accurate measure of the system's performance can be achieved. Samples that do not contain either parasite which can act as a control would be a useful addition. Additionally the two samples that contained Plasmodium vivax parasites were both poorly prepared, which could be caused as a result of either poor spreading techniques, water contamination, inadequate or late fixation or slow drying in humid conditions (Houwen, 2000).

There is still much work to do before the prototype system developed for this project could be used as a medical diagnosis tool, however as a proof of concept system most of the software and hardware components perform well.

6 References

Barber, P. (2005). Make your own automated microscopy system. Gray Cancer Institute, pages 1–11.

Chapelle, O., Haffner, P., and Vapnik, V. N. (1999). Support vector machines for histogram-based image classification. *Neural Networks, IEEE Transactions on*, 10(5):1055–1064.

Houwen, B. (2000). Blood film preparation and staining procedures. *Laboratory Hematology*, 6(1):1–7.

Katsadoraki, M. and Bugmann, G. (2012). Medical Diagnostic Robot, Plymouth University.

Likar, B. and Pernus, F. (2000). Retrospective shading correction of microscopical images.

Maitra, M., Gupta, R. K., and Mukherjee, M. (2012). Detection and Counting of Red Blood Cells in Blood Cell Images using Hough Transform. *International Journal of Computer Applications*, 53(16):13–17.

Milne, L. M., Kyi, M. S., Chiodini, P. L., and Warhurst, D. C. (1994). Accuracy of routine laboratory diagnosis of malaria in the United Kingdom. *Journal of clinical pathology*, 47(8):740–742.

Perocheau, K. (2012). Malaria Detection: Technical Report, Plymouth University.

Savkare, S. S. and Narote, S. P. (2011). Automatic detection of malaria parasites for estimating parasitemia. *International Journal of Computer Science and Security (IJCSS)*, 5(3):310.

Uc-Cetina, V., Brito-Loeza, C., and Ruiz-Pina, H. (2013). Chagas Parasites Detection through Gaussian Discriminant Analysis. *Abstraction & Application*, pages 6–17.

World Health Organization (2011). World Malaria Report 2011. World Health Organization.

World Health Organization (2013), "Chagas disease (American trypanosomiasis). Fact sheet number 340", www.who.int/mediacentre/factsheets/fs340/en/ (Accessed 12 August 2013)

Yuen, H. K., Princen, J., Illingworth, J., and Kittler, J. (1990). Comparative study of Hough transform methods for circle finding. *Image and Vision computing*, 8(1):71–77.

System Integration for Service Robot

J.Dauneau and G.Bugmann

School of Computing and Mathematics, Plymouth University, Plymouth, UK
e-mail: guido.bugmann@plymouth.ac.uk

Abstract

ButlerBot is an experimental robot, which aims to assist waiters during events, as a runner could do. Previously developed in 2007, this project saw its complexity increased through numbers of independent developments made for Masters projects and internships. At the start of the project 2013, those developments had to be integrated in a single environment, as to get an operational platform. In the same time, an important recast of the motion of the prototype had to be done, in addition with other communication systems, as to make its behaviour controllable, efficient, and sustainable in the time.

Keywords

Butlerbot, Graphical Developer Interface, I2C, Serial Com, Balancing control.

1 Introduction

Butler is a robotic platform created in 2006 by a Master student for his final year project (Railhet, 2007). This platform was dedicated to assist waiters during cocktails and events, to serve drinks as a runner could do. This project was a way to offer an unusual animation in a populated environment, by the presence of a robot offering a diverting way to serve cocktails.

From challenges in US as Robogames exposing robot bartenders (Robogames, 2013), to concrete realizations as the BaR2D2 (Price, 2013), this project is fully in line with a favourable context oriented towards assistance systems for the next years, as reported by the International Federation of Robotics (PBT Consulting, 2011).

The purpose of this paper is to give a presentation of the behaviour control of ButlerBot. Starting from the IMU, and going all along the process until the command of the wheels.

2 General description of the device

The balancing system is made of four parts, having the following specifications:

- The IMU, located under the tray, containing a basic code delivering raw data for the Pitch and the Roll. The data used are the gyroscopic values.

- The CM5, containing an Atmega 128, receiving those values, formatting them, and forwarding to the controller board.

- The Main board, or the controller board, receiving those values from the CM5, and adapting the motion of the robot with the formula described later.

An important aspect of this device is the need of synchronization in the process. Since the CM5 and the Main board communication protocols are based on interruptions, a prioritization is needed as to be sure that data are not lost. In our case, all remote commands are of maximum priority, and stop the reading of the sensors ; the second level contains all sensors and internal functions, which are basically scheduled in a main loop.

Part of the program aims to ensure that the size, the contain and the frequency of those readings are conformed. In the case of an unexpected error, the program breaks, reduces the speed if any, and waits for another packet.

In complement, we have to recall that the angles of the Pitch and Roll returned by the IMU are in fact integrated angular velocities, requiring "the continuous approximation of the change in the gyroscope readings" (Roberts, 2013). This part of the conversion is made in the controller of the IMU, located in "*AdcManager.h*", in the *GyroRoll_Process()* function. It basically aims to apply a new integrated value to the previous result for each new reading.

3 Balancing system

The control of the balance was a large part of the project. The objective aimed to develop a function able to counter-balance the natural tilt of the robot during the motion, or even a shock.

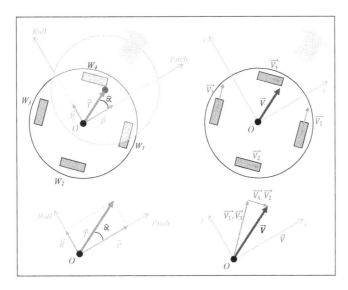

Figure 1: Mathematical approach of a tilt and recovery

Considering a tilt $\vec{T}$ (in red), composed by the sum of the Pitch $\vec{P}$ and the Roll $\vec{R}$, the aim of the function is to produce a proportional speed $\vec{V}$ in the same direction. The vector $\vec{V}$ will therefore be the resulting of the sum of the vectors $\vec{V_1}$, $\vec{V_2}$, $\vec{V_3}$ and $\vec{V_4}$ of each wheel.

The approach chosen to realise this function was based on assumptions that we describe here.

1. Measure of the length of the vector $\vec{V}$, with a simple Pythagoras formula:

(1) $V = \sqrt{P^2 + R^2}$

This will give us the intensity of the fall, and therefore define if the fall has to be countered, depending the threshold that we will see later.

2. Get the angle $\hat{\alpha}$ of the fall, related to the main axis of the robot. We use for that a trigonometric relation between the Pitch and the roll described here:

(2)

$$
\begin{cases}
\alpha = \tan^{-1}\left(\dfrac{Roll}{Pitch}\right) & , for\ (Pitch > 0) \\[2mm]
\alpha = \dfrac{\pi}{2} & , for\ (Pitch = 0\ and\ Roll > 0) \\[2mm]
\alpha = \dfrac{3\pi}{2} & , for\ (Pitch = 0\ and\ Roll < 0) \\[2mm]
\alpha = \pi + \tan^{-1}\left(\dfrac{Roll}{Pitch}\right) & , for\ (Pitch < 0)
\end{cases}
$$

3. Once the angle and the distance are identified, it is to apply a trigonometric formula as to get the speed to apply for each wheel. It is basically a projection of the fall on each axis of the plan, as described in Picture 2.

(3) $W_1 = \cos\left(\alpha + \dfrac{\pi}{4} + \dfrac{\pi}{2}\right) = \cos\left(\alpha + \dfrac{3\pi}{4}\right)$

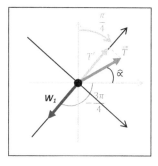

Figure 2: Calculation of the speed of the Wheel

Once the speed of each wheel is calculated, they are added to the initial speed of the robot, which could be defined remotely by the user in terms of speed or distance. The final system of equation for the control of the balancing will eventually be:

$$
(4)
\begin{cases}
V_1 = V_{Remote} + V \times F \times \cos\left(\alpha + \dfrac{3\pi}{4}\right) \\[2mm]
V_2 = V_{Remote} + V \times F \times \cos\left(\alpha - \dfrac{3\pi}{4}\right) \\[2mm]
V_3 = V_{Remote} + V \times F \times \cos\left(\alpha - \dfrac{\pi}{4}\right) \\[2mm]
V_4 = V_{Remote} + V \times F \times \cos\left(\alpha + \dfrac{\pi}{4}\right)
\end{cases}
$$

The program goes through the following steps:

- Receive the values of the IMU via an interruption. This task is to receive a complete packet from the USART1, which includes the control of the packet in terms of size and header.

- Split the packet in five values, as to get Pitch, Roll, Vector Angle, Fore acceleration, Side acceleration, but only the Pitch and the Roll will be used.

- Apply the tilt to the remote initial motion of the robot, which implies to add for each wheel the recovery speed to the remote speed already stored in the *RobotStatus* structure.

- Apply the speed with *SetSpeed()* , enable the Interruptions for the USART1, and break the loop.

4 Communication system

A serial communication device has been used to control the motion of the robot. This system was based on a USB-to-Serial device, connected to the USART0 of the main embedded board of Butler.

Since this device is connected to the USB port, the first step is to connect and set up the port as to allow the device to send and receive data through a buffer created for the purpose. In our case, the settings are:

1. Create a file buffer on the COM2, in read and write

2. Baud rate at 57,600

3. No parity

4. Byte size set to 8 bits

5. One stop bit for each packet

The result is an object, containing both the constructor detailed above, and the functions used to receive and send data through the buffer. The function to send data has the specificity to split the packet, depending its length. The reason was that the size of the buffer is limited to 30Bytes, and our objective is to anticipate any size of packet.

It has been necessary to create a dictionary of functions based on Tags, as to format the packets described here:

- Packet for a Distance-Angle command: for a command Distance-Angle.

<	[O]	00000	00000	00000	>
Start of Packet	TAG for command	X	Y	Angle	End of Packet
		first char could be "-" for negative value			

- Packet to switch from speed to distance control motion.

<	[M]	1/0	>
Start of Packet	TAG for command	Activation (1) / Deactivation (0) of the command	End of Packet

- Packet for a Speed command: the purpose of this command is to send a specific speed to each motor. This value can go up to 1,023 (cf. code "motors.c").

<	[C]	00000	00000	00000	00000	>
Start of Packet	TAG for command	Motor1	Motor2	Motor3	Motor4	End of Packet
		first char could be "-" for negative value				

The program inside the Atmega proceeds to a split of the packet received, and sends the values of the motors to the robot by using when needed the function *SetSpeed()* or *SetWantedPosition()*.

5 Conclusion and future

All those researches have contributed to the reinforcement of a Butler, initially not moving, as to make it again operational and offering a starting point for future researches. The results obtained in the communications, the sensors and the balancing system afford us to be confident in the fact that this project is back on track, and fully controllable in its motion, via the remote distance and speed control implemented in the GDI, extended for the purpose.

In the future, some axis of improvement could be the start of new researches topics. The motion system is today based on a instantaneous speed control, but could be oriented to an acceleration motion, which would be more "human friendly" than the jumps it made during the tests. In addition, the ordering system should (must?) be improved as to be fully dynamical and integrated in the GDI. A GDI which is to be improved as well in terms of processor and memory consumption, which could be a limit in some cases.

6 References

PBT Consulting, 2011. *Outlook for robotics and automation for 2011 and beyond are excellent says expert.* [Online] Available at: http://tommytoy.typepad.com/tommy-toy-pbt-consultin/2011/06/outlook-for-robotics-and-automation-for-2011-and-beyond-are-excellent-says-expert-.html [Accessed 07 08 2013].

Price, J., 2013. *Official Website of Bar2D2.* [Online] Available at: http://www.jamiepricecreative.com/bar2d2.html [Accessed 12 08 2013].

Railhet, S., 2007. *ButlerBot Service Robot,* Plymouth: University of Plymouth.

Roberts, S., 2013. *Gyroscopes and Accelerometers on Bipedal Walking Robot,* Plymout: University of Plymouth.

Robogames, 2013. *BarBot.* [Online] Available at: http://robogames.net/barbot.php [Accessed 10 08 2013].

Texas Instrument, 2012. *8-Bit, 8-Channel Sampling, Analog-to-Digital Converter with I2C™ Interface.* Dallas: Texas Instrument.

Web Usability and User Behaviour:
The Security of Passwords

C.M.Freeman and B.V.Ghita

Center for Security, Communications and Network Research,
Plymouth University, Plymouth, United Kingdom
e-mail: info@cscan.org

Abstract

This research aimed to find a relationship between usability of websites and password setting behaviours. More specifically, it aimed to identify whether or not there was a link between guidance given on password setting and the strength of the password set. The way in which this was carried out was to develop three differing versions of the same website with varying degrees of usability; both general and security usability. Participants were asked to register on a version of this website in order to create a username and password which would be used for analysis. Once participants had registered on the website they were asked to complete a survey asking them about their experience with the website they were presented.

Data from the website and survey was analysed to find some interesting results including evidence that suggests that password guidance is actively looked for when creating passwords, that language does not impact the response given to security messages, that IT experience affects password setting behaviours, and most noticeably that guidance given during password creation improves the strength of the password set.

Keywords

Usability, Security, Passwords, Password Strength, Password Guidance

1 Introduction

Website registration is common place with most online vendors and in general, users have to create usernames and passwords in order to maintain their online accounts with these organisations. With this method of authentication being the most popular online (Devilliers, 2010, Jali et al. 2009), behaviour of users when creating online accounts need to be that of caution and care. The best way for users to protect themselves is to keep their information secure by using a strong password that cannot be easily compromised.

This research aims to establish a link between information presented to the users and their behaviour on an arbitrary website. The information presented will help to determine whether or not guidance on password creation affects the strength of the password set.

2 The Problematic Password

Password creation is common practice online as most e-commerce websites require users to register before they can purchase anything. Good password practices should be common sense but there is a plethora of information and guidance about password creation on the internet.

2.1 Guidance

There is a lot of information on how to set a good password online, and in a lot of cases the websites on which users are registering have guidance available. The adoption of this is not continuous though, as the level of guidance varies dramatically from vendor to vendor.

In some cases where password practices and guidance are briefed to users, it is not always enforced as well as it could be. For example, password guidance available from Information Week advises users to create strong passwords, to use different passwords for all accounts and to change them regularly (Casey, 2012). However, they do not advise users to use different passwords when changing them, so users might use a variation of the same password. This is dangerous as if an old password is compromised, it would be easy to guess the new password by changing a small element of the known password. Users who know all the risks and security reasons for adhering to good password practices do not always behave the way they know they should because there are just too many passwords to remember. It is common place for users who set a difficult password to use it on every single online account (Sophos found a third of their respondents used the same password, 2009). This means that all accounts could be compromised if that one password was acquired.

Guidance given can be as straight forward as not writing down a password, not sharing a password, not using the same password more than once and ensuring that passwords are changed at regular intervals. In 2009, usernames and passwords of over 10,000 Windows Live Hotmail accounts were posted online. The top password (used 64 times in total) was "123456" (Acunetix, 2009). Using CSCAN's password strength checker (CSCAN, 2013) the strength of this password was checked and the result was frightening. The length of the password was quite short and would take a computer less than a week to guess it. The password was in position 2 of the top 10,000 passwords (SplashData, 2012). The password could be instantly guessed as it is in the most common password lists

In spite of all the warnings about weak passwords, people still use them. The password "123456" is not only easy to remember, but very easy to input at speed on a keyboard which may be part of the reason why it is so common.

Guidance can be presented in many ways; as an information blurb on the site to be read before setting a password, as a dynamic strength meter as the password is typed, or as information about the password when it is has been set (i.e. this password is not acceptable because). Password meters seem to have been increasing in popularity over the years. Research was carried out by the University of California who found that the presence of password meters yielded significantly stronger passwords

(Schwartz, 2013). The caveat on this research appeared to be that this only had an effect on website accounts that users perceived to be important. For accounts that were perceived as unimportant to the user, the password strength meters presence appeared to have little impact and weak passwords were still generated. In reality, this makes sense. If a website is perceived as unimportant to a user then they are less cautious about protecting it from misuse. When in best practice users are meant to have a single separate password for each account, it seems pointless to waste precious memory storage for complex passwords on sites that are unimportant.

2.2 Problems

One of the common problems users find when creating passwords is making it memorable. Very strong passwords of a certain length with a mixture of upper and lower case letters, numbers and punctuation are quite difficult to remember which can mean that some people create them but write them down which compromises their security.

When passwords are difficult to remember and have not been written down it can often mean a lot of administration on the vendor's side for sending reminder passwords or new passwords to users when they are forgotten. A survey on passwords found that 88% of respondents had to reset their password in the last two years (CSO, 2006).

The use of browsers password facility enables users to forget their passwords entirely for websites when accessing them from the same computer. This does mean however, that when these accounts are accessed from different machines, users will need to remember, reset or request their password for each of the websites.

In best practice, users should not use the same password on multiple websites. This is great in theory but in practice makes it very difficult to remember passwords for all online accounts. In these cases it is common for people to have a selection of passwords which are used for all accounts. A survey completed by Symantec in 2010 of over 400 people found that 45% of them have a few passwords and alternate between them (Symantec, 2010). A similar survey on passwords completed by Sophos found that a staggering 33% of respondents used the same password for all of their accounts and that 48% alternate between a few (Sophos, 2009).

In cases where people genuinely use a different password for each account, it could be that these people have written them down. In the same Symantec survey, 23% of respondents used their browser to keep track of their passwords, 18% made a note of them either electronically or on paper, 33% used password management software and 59% used their memory. In the case where memory was used, a hypothesis might be that users used the same password for all accounts but prefix or affix it with the name of the account, i.e. "Hotmail_pwd" and "Facebook_pwd". Although it is best practice to have different passwords for each account, if the users' password setting strategy is cracked, then all accounts can be compromised.

Password best practice also encourages users to keep passwords secure and not to share them, but the Symantec survey showed that an astonishing 43% of respondents had shared their passwords.

3 Experiment Design

Three different variations of the same website were created which allowed users to complete three specific tasks; register on the website, create a username and password, and to log in with these details in order to submit some feedback.

The websites were designed in such a way that they would cover good and bad usability as well as good and bad security usability features. The website was designed in conjunction with a PhD psychology research student was also interested in the effects of usability on security. Minor differences in the website versions were made to allow for different design features to be analysed in conjunction with user behaviour. The guidance on password setting was different on one of the websites.

Figure 1: Password guidance and strength meter found on PP and MP

The websites were named to reflect these differences, below is the breakdown:

1. Plus Plus; Good usability, good security usability (referred to as PP throughout)

2. Plus Minus; Good usability, bad security usability (referred to as PM throughout)

3. Minus Plus; Bad usability, good security usability (referred to as MP throughout)

Good Security Usability	Bad Security Usability
Password guidance: explanation, do's & don'ts, password strength meter and specific feedback	No password guidance other than advising user to choose a strong password
Insecure data transmission message clearly understandable to all participants regardless of prior knowledge	Insecure data transmission message written in technical terms

Users were not made aware which version they were accessing, but the version name was stored in the database linked to the website. Participants were sent a link to the survey which detailed the experiment for the participant and asked them to click a link which would direct them to the website in order to complete the tasks. When selecting the link, the database behind the website generated the name of the website to be accessed depending on which version of the website was last accessed. Participants were then asked to complete the tasks as detailed on the website, making a note of their unique participant ID displayed to them on the website. Once the tasks were completed on the website, they were informed to return to the survey to answer questions about their interaction.

The survey was mainly focussed on the usability and trust questionnaires WAMMI and SCOUT. As well as these questionnaires, there were demographical questions designed to find out from participants their age and IT experience which might be relevant when looking at the data for analysis. Participants were also asked about their password setting behaviours but this was an optional question.

4 Results

4.1 Password Strength Analysis

Password analysis was completed on the information gathered from the websites. The following results (rounded to whole numbers) were found when looking at the passwords.

For complete registrations (i.e. those that were not abandoned part way through):

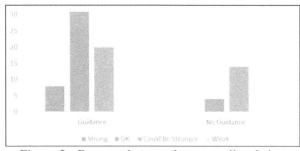

Figure 2: Password strength across all websites

- Websites with guidance had 14% "Strong" passwords versus 0% "Strong" passwords where guidance was not given

- Websites with guidance had 53% "OK" passwords versus 22% "OK" passwords where guidance was not given

- Websites with guidance had 34% "Could Be Stronger" passwords versus 78% "Could Be Stronger" passwords where guidance was not given

- None of the websites received any "Weak" passwords.

The original objective in relation to this data was to "identify whether guidance on password creation affect the strength of the password given". Looking at the information obtained from the websites, it is concluded that there is a significant difference between the numbers of passwords of a better strength in the versions where guidance was given. Having interviewed a handful of participants who took part in this study, the general feedback was that it was the strength meter which made the user aware of the strength of the password they had set. In all cases that were discussed, users reported that they did not read the bullet pointed information about password creation as there was too much to read, but that the strength meter enforced the password to be of a certain strength, so they "kept typing until the colour changed". 17% of passwords collected were suffixed with "1" and 57% of passwords were suiffixed with a number of some sort. In at least two instances, participants reported that they had changed the password they were originally using as the password strength meter was telling them that the password was weak. It is interesting to note that on the website where no password guidance was given, that there were no "Strong" passwords set. This speaks volumes in relation to this objective.

4.2   Password Guidance Analysis

During the survey completed after the interaction with the website, users were asked what they thought about how easy it was to set a good password, and whether they thought enough guidance was given. For the website versions PP and MP (where guidance was given which included a password strength meter), 82% of participants that answered the question agreed that it was easy to set a good password and 92% agreed that there was sufficient password guidance. For the website version PM (where no guidance was given) only 50% of participants that answered the question agreed it was easy to set a good password but a staggering 89% stated that there was not sufficient guidance to choose a good password. This information indicates that users were looking for guidance to set the password, but also that this guidance was then used to be able to set a good password.

5   Conclusions and the Future

There are numerous password strength meters online, and one of the top hits on Google is a password analyser provided by The Password Meter. The web page is full of guidance on how to set a good password and best practice for doing so. It also has a dynamic password strength meter which, when typed in, changes its display to reflect the score of the password typed. A score is given for different characteristics of a good password and a colour is assigned to reflect the strength. This is similar to the password checker offered by Microsoft, which also has guidance and a strength meter that dynamically changes its display depending on the password being typed.

The password checkers available from CSCAN, Microsoft and Password Meter all appear to do the same job. They provide very similar guidance for setting a strong password, but calculate the strength of the password in different ways. The passwords collected in this research were analysed through each of the meters and the findings are below:

	Password Meter	CSCAN	Microsoft
Very Weak	17%	22%	0%
Weak	21%	19%	69%
Medium	26% (Good)	52%	16%
Strong	22%	6%	16%
Best	14% (Very Strong)	0%	0%

Figure 3: Comparison of password ratings for passwords collected, across selection of password checkers (rounded to whole numbers)

This analysis shows that a password which may be seen as strong (or a similar descriptive term) on one of the password checker websites might be seen as average on another. At a quick glance it appears that the checker provided by Microsoft is stricter on passwords than the other two. No official weighting system exists (The Password Meter, 2013) which does not help with offering guidance to users as a more consistent approach should be identified. A suggestion for future work or research is to investigate a formal weighting system which could be seen as the official standard across all websites for password analysis.

Conclusions can be made about the work completed and its relevance to the world of web development, usability and security in relation to password creation behaviour. Guidance given to users during registration processes for creating passwords, does have an impact on the strength of the password set. The caveat to this conclusion is that the guidance needs to be processed quickly by the user, so a dynamic password strength meter is the best method for doing this.

The starkest finding from this research has been the simple fact that by utilising a relatively simple control on a website, which will analyse a password and dynamically change its appearance to the user for instant feedback, can have a phenomenal impact on users' behaviour when setting a password. A recommendation therefore would be that all web developers utilise these off the shelf controls (or develop them themselves) in order to achieve stronger passwords for their user base. It is not only in the interest of the user that their accounts are protected, but also for the vendor and its reputation. A foot note to this recommendation is that this would be best implemented after a standard weighting system is created and deployed internationally as a recognised standard to enforce consistency between websites.

6 Acknowledgements

This research study was designed in conjunction with Nina Bär, a PhD psychology student who conducted a similar version of the research in Germany. Shirley Aitkinson and Paul Dowland provided support with deploying the research websites on the Plymouth University web servers. Bogdan Ghita supervised this research project.

7 References

Acunetix (2009), "Statistics from 10,000 leaked Hotmail passwords", http://www.acunetix.com/blog/news/statistics-from-10000-leaked-hotmail-passwords/, (Accessed 13/02/2013)

Casey, K. (2012), "9 Password Security Policies for SMBs", Information Week, http://www.informationweek.com/smb/security/9-password-security-policies-for-smbs/232500320 (Accessed 02/08/2013)

CSCAN (2013), "Rate your password with Plymouth University", http://www.cscan.org/passwordstrength/, (Accessed 14/02/2013)

CSO (2006), "Those Pesky Passwords", http://www.csoonline.com/article/221733/those-pesky-passwords, (Accessed 13/02/2013)

Devillers, M. M. A. (2010), "Analyzing Password Strength", *Technical report*, Radboud University Nijmegen.

Jali, M. Z., Furnell, S. M., Dowland, P.S. (2010), "Assessing image-based authentication techniques in a web-based environment", *Information Management & Computer Security*, Volume 18 Issue 1, pp43-53.

Microsoft, "Password Checker", https://www.microsoft.com/en-gb/security/pc-security/password-checker.aspx (Accessed 01/06/2013)

Schwartz, M.J. (2013), "How Password Strength Meters Can Improve Security", *Information Week*, http://www.informationweek.co.uk/security/management/how-password-strength-meters-can-improve/240155209, (Accessed 05/06/2013)

Sophos (2009), "Security at risk as one third of surfers admit they use the same password for all websites, Sophos reports", http://www.sophos.com/en-us/press-office/press-releases/2009/03/password-security.aspx, (Accessed 13/02/2013)

SplashData (2012), "When 'Most Popular' isn't a good thing : worst passwords of the year and how to fix them", http://splashdata.com/splashid/worst-passwords/ , (Accessed 09/07/2013)

Symantec (2010), "Password Survey Results", http://www.symantec.com/connect/blogs/password-survey-results, (Accessed 13/02/2013)

The Password Meter, "Test Your Password", http://www.passwordmeter.com/, (Accessed 09/07/2013)

Network Security Monitoring
on Small Business Networks

J.Gammon-Loud and P.S.Dowland

Center for Security, Communications and Network Research,
Plymouth University, Plymouth, United Kingdom
e-mail: info@cscan.org

Abstract

Computer networks lie at the heart of modern society; they enable the transfer of unimaginable amounts of data over vast distances and as a result have created the global marketplace of e-commerce and online business transactions that we see today. The increase in computing power and networking speeds in recent years has created a monumental paradigm shift in almost every aspect of business as they allow for greater and greater levels of productivity and interconnectivity. As a result of this, computer networks are vital for the development and survival of almost all modern businesses big and small. The aim of the research conducted in this paper is to investigate the problems caused by poor network security monitoring in smaller business networks and to produce a software tool that can help to mitigate some of these problems.

Keywords

Network security, security monitoring, vulnerability scanners, SNMP, Syslog, HiveMind

1 Introduction

As the degree to which businesses rely upon computer networks increases, the need to protect them deepens. Large corporations are spending an ever increasing amount of money to secure their networks and smaller businesses cannot compete. This leaves them easy targets for the hackers that want to attack them for financial gain or corporate espionage. The severity, frequency and impact of cyber-attacks is on the rise; last year 74% of small businesses experienced a malicious security incident (PWC, 2012) with total industry losses amounting to billions in the UK alone. Despite this, CSI (2011) reports that over 43% of organisations spend less than 5% of their total IT budget on security.

This paper will look at the security problem in small business networks with the aim of producing a piece of software that can help to mitigate some of these problems. The specific area of focus is on network security monitoring, why it is of particular concern to small businesses and what can be done to improve the situation.

2 The Problem

There are an endless number of threats facing business networks; with motivations such as financial gain and corporate espionage business networks are a favourite target for hackers. Once they have accessed a network the hacker will usually be aiming either to capture the network traffic itself or to gain access to hosts on that network. In order for a host to remain secure the administrator must ensure that each machine has up to date software and appropriate well configured endpoint security software (Vacca, 2010).

As well as human hackers attempting to gain entry to networks and endpoints, there are also less obvious threats such as malware that will attempt to spread to hosts automatically and even internal users that will misuse their privileges to steal or destroy data (Yeh and Chang, 2007). No matter what the threat, proper monitoring is important in order to find possible vulnerabilities and prevent possible future attacks, to detect attacks that may be occurring right now in order to stop them and to find where attacks have already occurred to ensure that any security holes are fixed against future attack.

During this project there were a number of key security threats that were found to be preventable when the administrator has enough information about the network and its hosts. Problems such as distributed denial of server (DDoS), port scanning and traffic sniffing were studied to consider how they may be mitigated with the use of proper network security monitoring.

In order to analyse how security can be improved through better monitoring tools, existing tools and techniques were analysed; tools such as vulnerability scanners, simple network management protocol (SNMP) and Syslog were analysed for the strengths and weaknesses. The research found some significant gaps and weaknesses in the current solutions such as high cost, complex interfaces, complex reports poor security, and narrow scope.

From the research it is clear that current solutions in security monitoring are inadequate and that an easier and cheaper tool targeted at smaller networks is needed. Having studied some of the tools for network monitoring and security monitoring, it is clear that they all have advantages and disadvantages. Many of them seem to be more focused on large business networks, if an alternative could be developed that used their advantages without the disadvantages that make them inaccessible to smaller business networks, it could be an extremely effective tool.

By combining the scanning abilities of vulnerability scanners with the logging and aggregation abilities of syslog and SNMP, a tool could be created that would be able to keep the network administrator up to date with important characteristics and events on the network, without the overwhelming and complex interface that often comes with this functionality. This tool could fulfil an extremely important role on the network by allowing the administrator to monitor their network quickly and easily for important events and security risks.

3   The Solution

Using information about both the security threats and current solutions, it was possible to derive a list of requirements for a solution to the problem of poor network security monitoring in small business networks. The following requirements were identified:

The software should:

- Aid network administrators by providing the administrator with information about hosts on their network
- Provide the administrator with alerts when a host is a risk of attack
- Provide a user friendly interface allowing administrators to view important alerts or general host information with minimum effort
- Allow the administrator to view a brief history of alerts and reports to see how the network has changed
- Allow the administrator to customise which kind of alerts they wish to receive
- Consist of a client application to gather data and a server application for the collection, analysis and presentation of reports and alerts
- The system should use data from hosts and from network-based scans to produce more accurate host information

The resulting software tool was named HiveMind; a software system based on the idea of combining the benefits of network based vulnerability scanners with the client information of SNMP and the logging capabilities of SysLog. HiveMind uses data collected from a piece of client software running on each network host much like an SNMP agent and combines it with data from network based scans like a vulnerability scanner to produce reports and alerts which can help an administrator to stay informed about problems on their network. The software allows the administrator to see the history of reports to see how hosts on their network have changed over time, as well as alerting them when certain key changes happen to hosts.

The software measures key system characteristics as well as performance information and allows the administrator to monitor the status of processes of their choosing on the client. In a real network security incident, the information provided by the reporting of HiveMind can be used to alert the administrator to a wide range of threats; the performance information detailing the CPU and memory status of the host can be used to detect the symptoms of a botnet infection or other malware infections that use high numbers of system resources. The ability of the administrator to control which processes the host should monitor mean that the administrator can monitor the status of antivirus software in case malware or even the user disables it. The ability of the administrator to monitor the open ports of a host is very useful as it allows them to quickly and easily diagnose problems with firewall software, malware setting up listening ports as well as unauthorised and unsafe user behaviour such as torrenting. The monitoring of client MAC address can reveal MAC address spoofing, an important precursor to many hacking attempts or other malicious activity from a user or malware.

The above paragraph lists some of the ways in which HiveMind may be useful in securing a real network; it works by providing the administrator with much of the information they may need without having over-complicated and lengthy reports. The following discussion explains how HiveMind solves many of the problems found with existing security tools.

One of the problems stated with classical vulnerability scanners is that they can be very difficult to use; with lengthy reports and complex interfaces for setting up and using the tools (Holm, 2012 and Stuart, 2005). This problem was addressed in HiveMind and as a result it uses very simple alert and report forms that present only very basic information. The settings menus on both the client and the server software are also very simple and contain only a few important controls. The result of this combined with the standard Windows form layout provided by visual studio and C# make HiveMind an easy and intuitive piece of software to use.

Another issue with vulnerability scanners discussed by Welberg (2008) was that many of them do not use aggregation techniques, leaving the administrator with a fairly narrow view of the system. This problem was addressed in HiveMind with the addition of the server and client side monitoring techniques. This system allows the administrator to view reports and alerts that have been generated using aggregated data from more than one source. This may increase the accuracy of the data in some circumstances, however, this is not a perfect implementation of the aggregated system as it does still rely very heavily on information gathered directly from the client.

One further problem with vulnerability scanners as noted by Stuart (2005) is that their scan data can have a limited scope; only looking for problems related to unpatched software. This problem was addressed during the design of HiveMind by providing a more diverse range of information that could be relevant to the security of the system. The downside to this approach is that it requires some interpretation of the reports by the administrator, the answer to this problem was to include alerts which explain to the administrator in plain English when there is a problem that they need to look at.

Another software solution that was considered during the design of HiveMind was simple network management protocol (SNMP) systems. HiveMind uses many of the characteristics of SNMP in that is uses the client-side agent to gather much of the information it uses, however, there were also some security problems with SNMP that needed to be addressed. As a result, HiveMind uses encrypted reports with replay protection and uses strong 256-bit AES encryption to protect the report information from attackers. It also uses a more simple interface and a more comprehensive logging technique than many SNMP systems.

The final tool used to produce the requirements for HiveMind was Syslog, a logging system that allows an administrator to collect data from around the network and store it for auditing and monitoring purposes. HiveMind uses some of this functionality in that it collects and logs information, but is improved in that it performs higher level processing on that information to produce reports per client and alerts when there is an urgent problem; this is something that Syslog does not provide. In addition to the additional functionality, HiveMind also provides additional security in the form of report encryption and customisable process gathering which overall makes it a more useful solution that Syslog alone.

4 Future Work

There are several areas in which, given more time, the project could have been taken further and the product could have been improved. The following is a list of areas that could have been developed further:

- Improved flexibility and customisability

- Increased number of monitored characteristics

- Improved alert system

- Improved logging capability

One of the main problems with the product is its rigidity, apart from the ability for the administrator to customise the monitored processes; no other aspects of the application can be changed. In order to improve usefulness for a more diverse range of networks it would be helpful to have the ability to customise which alerts you wish to receive. Furthermore, the addition of plugin style alert modules would be a great advantage; allowing quick and easy updates to the software as well as giving users the ability to write their own alert rules to suit their network would make the software much more useful in a greater number of situations.

Currently, the system monitors basic system information, given more time it would have been possible to include a greater number of host characteristics such as password checking, windows system event log checking and interfaces with antivirus software. All of these more advanced characteristics would improve the resolution of the reports giving the administrator a more clear view of the network.

Another problem with the current system is that the alert system is currently quite one dimensional, allowing the administrator to see the alerts only if they are sat at their desk looking at the server machine. It would be useful to add functionality such as email alerting or syslog event generation.

Finally, there is a problem with the current implementation in that it uses a fairly primitive approach to alert and report storage; it uses files to store this information and deletes them when they are no longer required. This approach is problematic for security auditing purposes and is also very insecure. The ideal approach to allow for more efficient logging, analysis and archiving would be to include a database system for the storage of reports and alerts. This could be implemented using a number of available database packages such as Oracle or MySQL and would allow the system to archive large volumes of past data for future auditing purposes. It would also enable greater use of relationships between reports and alerts which could both improve the efficiency of data processing and storage.

5   References

Beitollahi, H., and Deconinck, G. (2012). *Analyzing well-known countermeasures against distributed denial of service attacks.* Computer Communications. 35, pp.1312-1332.

Bhuyan, M. H., Bhattacharyya, D. K., and Kalita, J. K. (2011). *Surveying Port Scans and Their Detection Methodologies.* The Computer Journal 54 (10), pp.1565-1581.

Holm, H. (2012). *Performance of automated network vulnerability scanning at remediating security issues.* Computers & Security. 31 pp.164-175.

Lee, C.B., Roedel, C., and Elena, S. (2003). *Detection and Characterization of Port Scan Attacks. Technical Report,* University of California, San Diego, CA.

PWC. (2012). *Information Security Breaches Survey.* London: Price Waterhouse Cooper.

SANS. (2008). *Salary and Certification Survey.* Bethesda: SANS Institute.

Simoneau, P. (1999). *SNMP network management.* London: McGraw-Hill.

Stuart, A. (2005). *Network Security. A contemporary approach to network vulnerability assessment.* Network Security. 2005(4). pp.7-10.

Vacca, J.R. (2010). *Network and System Security.* Oxford: Elsevier.

Welberg, S.M. (2008). *Vulnerability management tools for COTS software - A comparison.* MBI. University of Twente

Whitman, M.E. and Mattord, H.J. (2011). *Principles of Information Security.* 4th ed. Boston: Cengage Learning.

Yeh, Q., and Chang, A.J. (2007). *Threats and countermeasures for information system security: A cross-industry study.* Information & Management. 44, pp.480-491.

Kinect Based Mapping and Navigation of Differential Drive Autonomous Vehicle

N.Muniyappa Devaraju and D.Livingstone

School of Computing and Mathematics, Plymouth University, Plymouth, UK
e-mail: d.livingstone@plymouth.ac.uk

Abstract

The project is to design a prototype of holonomic differential drive autonomous vehicle. Develop an application for the system to generate a map of the given environment and navigate safely in the environment using the map, vision data and encoder information as reference. Differential drive vehicle is built using TETRIX components and established an electrical connection between motors, encoders, batteries, motor controller, and NXT brick. Programmed NXT brick to receive motor data and transmit encoder data for central unit (laptop) serially over Bluetooth. Effective communication is established between vehicle, central unit and vision system. Develop an application using ros libraries for mapping, driving and navigation of the vehicle. The hardware and application is calibrated and tested under the confined environment, for efficient mapping and navigation of the vehicle. Prototype of the differential drive was built. System was capable enough in generating a map of the testing environment and navigates in the environment referencing the map and sensor data effectively.

Keywords

Kinect Sensor, Navigation, Mapping, Depth Image, Autonomous Vehicle

1 Introduction

In this paper, several techniques are discussed and try to come out with a new approach of vision system for autonomous vehicle. Aim is to use the low cost electronics to design the effective machine vision system of the autonomous vehicle and study various techniques to improve the efficiency of the system in the given environment i.e. mapping localization and navigation functionalities of the vehicle. In this report, background of the autonomous is briefly discussed followed by methodology, evaluation and conclusion.

2 Background

Navigation of the autonomous vehicles is the challenging task in the field of mobile Robotics. Many researches are conducted on this topic from several years to develop a perfect navigation system for the autonomous vehicles. Driving the system autonomously in an unknown environment includes various sensor system and efficient algorithm. The types of navigation system are used across the globe to guide the autonomous vehicle.

Wire guidance system was traditionally used in the earlier stages of automation industries. The wire sensing device was attached at the bottom of the vehicle to detect the radio frequency transmitted by the wire that is placed under the ground (Wikipedia 2013).Guide tape navigation system use magnetic tape or color tape which is laid on the flour and the guiding system of the vehicle sense this tape using electromagnetic induction or light sensor and guide the vehicle to follow the tape (Wikipedia 2013). Laser target navigation is the recent guidance system used in autonomous robotics. The laser transmitter and receiver is mounted on the vehicle and made it to rotate over the vertical axis. Reflector Tapes or reflectors are mounted on the walls or pole as a reference points for the system. Vehicle reaches its destination by constantly updating its position with reference to preloaded map (Wikipedia 2013). Vision navigation is the kind of system which uses vision sensors to collect the location information. A vision sensor such as camera is used to record the features of the surroundings and guide the vehicle accordingly. No much modification in the environment is required to install this system (Wikipedia 2013). Vision system has more advantages, such as low cost of electronics, easy maintenance, less noise, rich in information.

Zhang et al. (2004) made the research on the visual navigation of autonomous vehicle based on path recognition system. In this project they developed a guide line recognition system using Hough transforms algorithm and by processing the input information, generated appropriate motor commands to guide the vehicle. Based on this path information they programmed to call different sub functions for straight and turn movement of the vehicle (Zhang et al. 2004). In the same way, Shi, W. and Samarabandu, j. (2006) designed corridor line detection for vision based indoor navigation using canny edge detection and Hough Transform to process image and extract corridor straight lines to differentiate the path from the side walls (Shi, W. and Samarabandu, j. 2006).

The next advancement in the vision system is using invariant land mark which can be easily detected by the camera and can accurately measure the vehicle position and orientation by extracting the embedded information from the landmark. Zheng, R. and Yuan, K. (2008) developed the unique 2D artificial landmark, which is called MR (Mobile Robot) code. It is a simple pentagon shape 2D structure which holds some BCH code in the (Zheng, R. and Yuan, K. 2008). Ye A. et al. (2012) use this code to build the vision navigation for autonomous guided vehicle. In their project the landmark was glued on the floor and by using tilted camera down the image of the landmark was processed (Ye A. et al. 2012).

3 Technology

3.1 Concept

Autonomous vehicle is a kind of vehicle which has a capability to drive by itself in the given environment, using preloaded information of the work area along with the sensor data collected from the environment. Depending on the level of autonomy the vehicle can be adapted for various fields such as industrial process automation, space vehicles, military applications, entertainment, domestic floor cleaners etc. higher level autonomous vehicle should have the ability to acquire all the information of the environment in which it is intended to function. Drive autonomously without any human interference. Perform desired functions with less errors and self recovery behaviors. Work in the safe areas by avoiding obstacles and not harming humans. In some situations it is also made to learn the environment and adapt to any changes in the surrounding to accomplish the given task.

Automatic guided vehicle will hold some information of its position and location in the given environment and plans the perfect path to reach the goal. initially to localize itself in the given world, vehicle uses its onboard sensors such as encoders, Global positioning system, Laser range detectors, infrared cameras, vision systems etc. the position system involves various algorithms to find vehicles position. Some of them are histogram filter(markov localization), particle filter(Monte Carlo localization) and even kalman filter, which helps in calculating location and orientation of the vehicle, so that the vehicle have knowledge of its own position and calculate proper plan to navigate in the environment safely and reach the goal. This is the most challenging task to accomplish and various methodologies and hardware configurations are used in different combinations to get accurate results.

However, main aim of this paper is to deliver an autonomous vehicle which is capable of driving around in the given environment and generate a 2D map of the environment using onboard depth camera. Later using the same map as reference, vehicle navigates autonomously in the environment to reach the user specified goal.

3.2   Hardware

The vehicle control system is mainly made up of a non-holonomic three wheel differential drive mobile base unit, built from Tetrix parts (TETRIX, 2013) and Hi-tech driver circuit (Motor Drive) (HI-Technic, 2013), NXT brick with RobotC firmware used to communicate between computer and Hi-tech driver over serial bus, Microsoft Xbox360 Kinect camera (Kinect, 2013), a computer (laptop), Two 3000 mAh high-current 12V nickel-metal hydride battery to power up kinect and Hi-tech drive. The prototype of the model is shown in Figure 1.

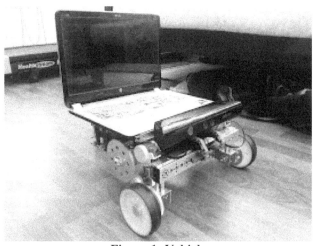

Figure 1: Vehicle

In the system, computer using ROS Openni libraries (OpenNI, 2013) receives depth information from the kinect mounted on mobile base via serial USB communication. This information is processed in the computer and respective control commands are produce to control to drive the vehicle.

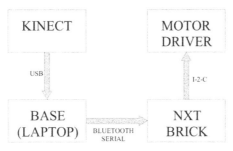

Figure 2: Block Diagram

Based on these commands motor velocities are produced and transmitted over serial Bluetooth to NXT brick. Brick then process the received data and transmit the same over I2C communication to Hi-tech drivers to change the pose and axis of the vehicle to track the identified human in front of the vehicle. The complete communication set up is shown in Figure 2.

3.3   Software

LEGO NXT brick (NXT, 2013) flashed with RobotC firmware (RobotC, 2013) and programmed to use has a mediator in between base unit and Hi technic motor controller because Hi technic controller can be driven easily by NXT brick. By this code compiled into the NXT brick, the vehicle is ready to accept the motor values and commands to drive the vehicle and provide appropriate encoder values to the base unit for further calculations of the vehicle position and orientation.

The base unit is the main processing unit which is a laptop running on Ubuntu operating system. The core application for this project is developed under ROS (Robot Operating System) libraries. ROS is an open-source, meta-operating system for various robot applications (ROS, 2013). It provides device drivers for various hardware's, node management, messages to interact between the nodes, various visualizing tools, package management, low level device control and more. It also provides tools and libraries for writing and running the code across multiple processors. The ROS graph is a runtime network of many nodes that are broadly coupled using the ROS communication protocol such as synchronous RPC type (RCP, 2013) communication over services, asynchronous streaming of information over topics, and its storage on a Parameter Server(ROS, 2013). Various nodes are developed under this unit.

Sensor node is written to fetch point cloud from the kinect sensor and process it to generate appropriate laser scans for 2D mapping and navigation purposes.

Odomtf node is developed to receive encoder values from the vehicle and generate odometric coordinate frame for the navigation system. This node also transform odom frame to base unit.

Drive node will receive linear and angular velocities and converts this twist message into respective motor velocities based on the mobile base width to cope with the differential drive system of the vehicle.

NXT node just transfers the motor velocities from the drive node and receives encoder value from the brick by communicating with the brick over Bluetooth serial.

NXT brick is used as a mediator to talk with Hi-tech driver. Thus the motor values is first transmitted to the brick over serial Bluetooth and later brick process these values and send it to each motor (left and right) respectively.

Transform nodes will transform all the coordinate frames, to define the relationship between the frames which helps for safe navigation of the vehicle.

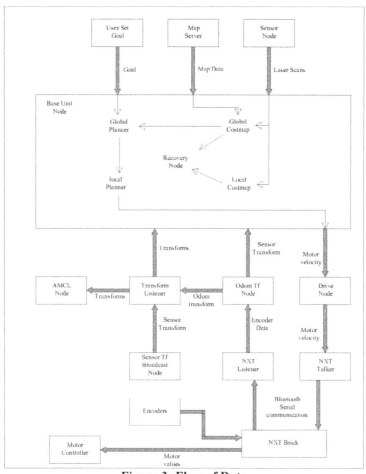

Figure 3: Flow of Data

Move base node is the core unit which generates motor commands by using sensor data, map and transforms. When the user set the goal in the map, this node will produce cost maps that hold obstacle information in it and by using this information, base planner function of the node will generate the planned path to reach the goal and produce appropriate motor values to drive the vehicle towards the goal and accomplish the task. During the drive, trajectories are formed ahead the vehicle to calculate and predict possible collision of the vehicle with the obstacle and choose the safest trajectory from it to generate the local plan. This local plan is to make sure the vehicle drive safely in the local area.

The flow of data processing is shown in Figure 3.

The vehicle model is designed to simulate and visualize the real world process. The graphical representation of the vehicle is shown in Fig 4 which is linked with all the coordinate frames of the real world process.

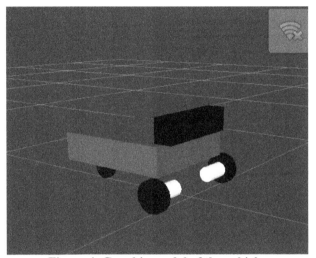

Figure 4: Graphic model of the vehicle.

4   Evaluation

A physical experiment is conducted in the home corridor. Motor speed for both angular and linear motion was set to minimum to avoid wheel slips. At first the vehicle was controlled manually all over the corridor to generate the 2D mad of the corridor as shown in the Figure 5.

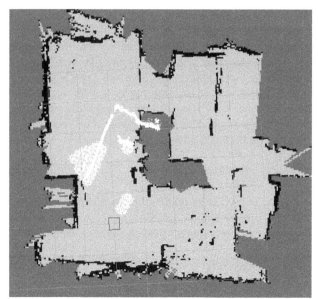

Figure 5: Generated map of house corridor.

When the complete map is generated the navigation and localization application are launched. Now the robot refer the generated map the compare it with the sensor data to identify its location in the corridor. For the application uses Monte Carlo technique by distribution random pose particles all over the place. Once the localization is achieved, the condensed particle will appear on the robot foot print. This can be visualized using visualization tool as shown in Figure 6.

Figure 6: Red spot is the particle cloud over the virtual robot model. Green spots are the obstacles and coloured area around the green is the inflation.

The performance and efficiency of the vehicle was tested by setting the goal on the map using visual tool and observed the path planning and obstacle avoidance behaviours of the vehicle.

The recovery behaviour of the vehicle was also observed when ever vehicle fails to track the path. In Figure 6 the green spots is the actual obstacle detected by cost maps and coloured area around it is the inflation around the obstacles to which the vehicle model should not coincide to make a safe drive.

5   Conclusion

The prototype of differential drive vehicle is designed using TETRIX parts and motors. Tested the vehicle to analyze its capable to generate the 2D map of the given environment using sensor data from kinect sensor, localize by itself using both map and sensor data and finally capable to reach user specified goal by navigating in the environment referencing the generated map and planning efficiently to avoid collision with obstacles while approaching towards the goal. Nevertheless with few errors like some inaccuracy in the generated map and wrong path calculation which depends on complexity, perfectness of the map. Odometric errors due to wheel slip; this should be improved in later versions. However the complete cost effective autonomous vehicle was built and tested its performance in the real world using less onboard low cost sensors.

6   References

HI-Technic (2013), "Motor Controller Specifications", http://www.legoeducation.us/etc/s upportFiles/TETRIX/739413/HiTechnicMotorControllerBriefv1.3.pdf (Accessed 14-05-2013)

Kinect (2013), "Microsoft Xbox Kinect", http://en.wikipedia.org/wiki/Kinect (Accessed 04-06-2013)

NXT (2013), "Lego Mindstroms NXT", http://en.wikipedia.org/wiki/Lego_Mindstorms_NXT (Accessed 14-05-2013)

OpenNI (2013), "OpenNI libraries for Kinect", http://www.ros.org/wiki/openni (Accessed 04-06-2013)

ROS (2013), "Robot Operating System", http://www.ros.org/wiki (Accessed 04-06-2013)

RobotC (2013), "RobotC for NXT", http://www.robotc.net (Accessed 14-05-2013)

RCP (2013), "Remote Procedure Call", http://en.wikipedia.org/wiki/Remote_procedure_call (Accessed 20-06-2013)

Shi, W. And Samarabandu, J. (2006) "Corridor Line Detection For Vision Based Indoor Robot Navigation", 1-4244-0038-4 2006 IEEE CCECE/CCGEI, Ottawa

TETRIX (2013), "TETRIX Kit For Student", http://www.tetrixrobotics.com (Accessed 14-05-2013)

Wikipedia (2013), "Automated guided vehicle", http://en.wikipedia.org/wiki/ Automated_guided_vehicle (Accessed at 27/08/1014)

Ye, A., Zhu, H., Xu, Z., Sun, C. and Yuan, K. (2012) "A Vision-Based Guidance Method for Autonomous Guided Vehicles", Proceedings of 2012 IEEE International Conference on Mechatronics and Automation August 5 - 8, Chengdu, China

Zheng, R. and Yuan, K. (2008) "MR Code for Indoor Robot Self-localization", Proceedings of the 7th World Congress on Intelligent Control and Automation, Chongqing, China

Zhang, H. B., Yuan, K., Zhou, Q., R., Mei S, Q. (2004) "Visual Navigation Of An Automated Guided Vehicle Based On Path Recognition", Proceedings of the Third International Conference on Machine Learning and Cybernetics, Shanghai, 26-29

WebAware: An Interactive Tool to Increase User Security Awareness

A.Newman and S.M.Furnell

Center for Security, Communications and Network Research,
Plymouth University, Plymouth, United Kingdom
e-mail: info@cscan.org

Abstract

Due to the increased popularity internet based products and services, phishing and social engineering attacks are becoming common within our daily lives. As a result, privacy and security can be considered highly important not only within the business sector, but also within home environments.

The following paper details the production of an interactive educational tool, based around the concept of increasing awareness within areas such as phishing, social engineering and system security.

Findings within the paper not only suggest that the produced software solution is an effective tool for user education, but also the majority of test users preferred this interactive learning over traditional methods. This paper also validates existing research based around attack demographics, performed during product testing. Due to user education being viewed more commonly as a necessary mitigation factor for security threats, the performed research could have a substantial impact within this area, with users employing more interactive education over traditional methods. .

Keywords

User awareness, security, phishing, social engineering, interactive systems

1 Introduction

The definition of social engineering differs from source to source with many security professionals in disagreement. Hadnagy (2011) describes social engineering as the act of manipulating an individual to perform an action that may or may not be in the "target's" best interest. This may include obtaining information, gaining access, or getting the target to take certain action. An example of this is described by CSO (2011), they explain that instead of attempting to find a security flaw or software vulnerability some attackers may simply pose as IT support staff and trick a user into divulging their password or other information.

Consequently, staff and user security awareness is becoming a critical factor within modern security policies and strategies. However while businesses are attempting to keep staff trained and aware, the same cannot be seen within home user environments. User training within this area is normally overlooked, meaning users could be highly susceptible without this type of awareness training. Symantec (2013) recently reported that one in 508.6 emails we're identified as phishing, 1 in 400 emails contained malware and that 2,256 malicious sites are blocked each day. These figures show users are subjected to this type of potentially damaging content on a daily basis. While many users could argue that they have suitable protection in place, it is important to note without suitable training users could still be susceptible due to outdated software packages, disabled services or even incorrect protection in place.

As identified above, phishing is clearly an issue for users. With millions of spam and phishing emails sent each day this is another area in which this paper will focus. Phishing can be defined as "the act of stealing personal information via the internet for the purpose of committing financial fraud"(Milletary, 2005). With more and more financial transactions moving to online sources and more users gaining easier access to the internet, it is clear how dangerous both these types of attacks can be to unaware individuals.

Finally, another key topic that will form part of this paper is general security awareness for users. Many users and particularly users lacking knowledge of Windows systems, are susceptible to a number of attacks that have simple countermeasures. These countermeasures can range from enabling the Windows firewall to use of complex security tools. While these system processes seem like common knowledge for many, a large number of users are not aware of the potential dangers of not taking these actions, or how to apply these changes. Therefore education of users in respect to social engineering and phishing attacks will form a key part of this project, in conjunction with education within topics such as basic system security and preventative measures against attacks.

2　Objectives

This paper, associated research and software solution have several key aims and objectives.

A key objective is to research current methods used to educate users, within this "security awareness" field. This requires research into current educational methods to increase security awareness. It also involves research based around current "interactive systems" that are used within user education. Finally research into user response to these educational systems will also be conducted.

Another objective is to view previous implementations of this type of system, through previous student projects and other system implementations (Anti-Phishing Phil). This requires research into previous implementations of educational systems allowing analysis of user feedback, this therefore allows the produced software solution to avoid possible implementation issues.

One other key objective is to produce a functioning educational tool to educate users. This objective requires that a system will implemented allowing a user to easily "pick up and play". This means that they should not need any prior knowledge of security attacks or security systems to play.

The final objective within this process is evaluation of the interactive system. This last aim of this project involves evaluation of the effectiveness of the produced solution and its ability to educate users. This will therefore require direct feedback and evaluation from users, some of which will test the system in a supervised environment, while others will simply have access to an online resource.

3   Existing Research and Previous Implementations

In the context of existing research into user education, there have been several different opinions by security professionals of its effectiveness at reducing phishing and social engineering risks. Kumaraguru et al (2009) explains that there is evidence to support the theory that user education is effective in the real world, especially in cases where the educational element is well designed. Gorling (2006) argues that user education however can be considered ineffective in real world systems. They go on to explain that even educated users are still unable to identify if a site is fraudulent even with the user of visual aids.

Plohmann et al. (2011) explain that user education can be an effective means to mitigate botnets and other security issues. They go on to explain that these security benefits can be divided into a number of categories. The first area that is described is education within malware systems. According to the report, education within malware spreading mechanisms can reduce the risk and prevent infections from drive-by infections, included in unsolicited email or caused by linked websites. It is also stated that this could improve awareness of other malware spreading mechanisms such as infections from untrusted removable media.

It is also described that education that emphasises the importance of security updates and keeping systems up to date will protect users from vulnerabilities that are commonly exploited by users. Information is also presented regarding password security, Plohmann et al. (2011) explains that increasing user education of password management will reduce the potential impact of attacks as they occur. Finally Plohmann et al. (2011) explains that education within the symptoms of system infection and guidance of how to treat an infection when it does occur, can minimize the damage experienced by users.

Within their research, Anandpara and Dingman (2007) explain that user education is not always effective. Their findings in their report show that traditional forms of education can increase the level of fear or concern among users, however this does not increase their ability to recognize phishing attacks.

Another element within reviewing the current state of the field is previous implementations of interactive systems to increase security awareness. One of these interactive systems is known as "Anti-Phishing Phil", the production of this system is described by Sheng et al. (2007) describing the purpose of this system as a game that teaches users good habits to avoid phishing attacks. Sheng et al. (2007) describes current phishing detection tools as ineffective stating that one tool could only identify 90% of phishing sites. This tool attempts to move away from autonomous processes, instead attempting to inform and educate users within the field of phishing attacks and how to detect them. The report outlines the design process of the software tool explaining game mechanics, story and technical specifications. The most important aspect of Sheng's (et al.) research in this case, is how effective an interactive system is in educating users. The report concludes that interactive systems can be an effective way of educating users, and that when coupled with learning science principles these materials can stimulate learning.

This research performed by Sheng et al. provides a backing for this type of project, meaning that the concept of interactive learning can be a successful method of education. This should hopefully be supported by my own findings during the testing and results phase.

Overall it is clear to see that there is a divide between security professionals within user security education and its effectiveness at reducing risk to users. However it should be noted that most of this research was performed using traditional methods of education, most commonly in the form of written materials. This type of user education and the associated results will greatly differ from the form of education presented within this final solution. Therefore the results presented within this paper are expected to differ in comparison with the results presented within previous research.

4   Implementation Aspects

4.1   Development Engine

While there are a vast number of development engines available for production of an interactive system. Due to both previous experience and the perceived benefits of its use, Unity was selected as the main engine for this project.

4.2   Language Development Language Selection

Selection of unity for a development engine imposed some limitations on the development language options within this project. The options for development of scripts within unity, fall to three languages, C#, Javascript and Boo.

Due to previous experience in C#, this language was therefore preferable in comparison with the others. While the syntax style is similar between C# and java, there are some advantages in its use, the main advantage being integration of LINQ enabling easy data query actions to be performed.

4.3   System Implementation

4.3.1   System Overview

Figure 1 shows an example desktop simulation level, this normally consists of multiple methods in which a user can complete the level (i.e. from the taskbar or control panel window). The aim of this game mode is to educate users in simple ways they can protect themselves, using software or hardware tools that are widely accessible. A large proportion of users for instance are unaware of the benefits of software or hardware firewalls, this game mode attempts to address this issue. Many of the other levels within this system follow a similar theme attempting to use different functionality to provide education within a number of areas. The next section describes these game modes and the potential impacts they can have upon the user awareness.

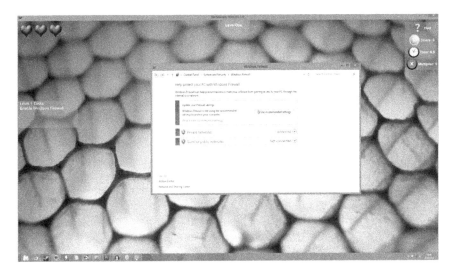

Figure 1: Example desktop simulation

4.3.2   Game Modes

Desktop Simulation – As previously discussed, this game mode involves a user completing tasks in attempt to educate them in general system security or using specific tools.

Question Levels – This game mode involves a user selecting the correct answer to a question based upon a number of options (multiple choice). This mode attempts to educate users in a number of areas dependant on the type of question.

URL Construction (Drag and Drop) – In this game mode a user can drag and drop named tiles, in an attempt to construct a phishing URL. This level attempts to educate users in how to spot these URLs, looking at areas such as extensions, subdomains and general URL syntax.

Spot the difference - This game mode attempts to educate users in spotting phishing scams that attempt to emulate legitimate websites. This game mode allows for users to spot spelling mistakes, lack of https indicator, as well as other options, which are common within phishing sites. The education provided by this game mode attempts to raise awareness of common factors that can be used to spot phishing emails or scams.

Phishing Emulation – Phishing emulation attempts to replicate a typical phishing site, demonstrating a scenario where a user could be asked for credentials or personal information. This game mode attempts to educate users in their response to phishing emails and sites, instead of further education of how to spot such attacks.

Find the Phish - The final game-mode attempts to educate users in how to effectively spot specific types of scam or phishing email. This mode simply asks a user to click the phishing email out a number of other options. This level is designed to be quick and easy to complete, while providing a basis of how to spot legitimate and illegitimate sites and emails.

5   User Evaluation and Testing

5.1   User Product Testing

Test Process:

The 18 test users were given unsupervised access to the interactive system with a basic set of instructions explaining how to load and play the game. These instructions were kept brief as it enabled a measure of the games effectiveness as a "pick up and play" solution. Once these test users had loaded the game and ran through the tutorial stage, they we're asked to run through the game a total of three times, each time they were asked to record their total score. Upon completing this system test, users were approached to give feedback regarding the systems "ease of use", its effect on their current knowledge of phishing and its effectiveness as a learning tool.

The first question within the questionnaire attempted to evaluate user's response to the system as a whole, attempting to gauge its impact on their approach to phishing and security. The results of this question shows that 77.78% of respondents felt that the system had a positive impact on their approach, while 22.22% felt that it did not. This figure supports the concept that it can be an effective educational tool as these users suggest.

The next question attempted to evaluate if users were supportive of this type of educational method, or prefer more traditional forms of education. The result was largely supportive of interactive educational systems with 88.88% of respondent's stating that they prefer interactive methods over traditional forms.

When asked to provide feedback regarding the games "ease of use", the feedback was largely positive. Most users (83.33%) indicated that they found the system easy to use with many giving particular comments that the tutorial and addition of help messages assisted them through their play-through. 16.6% of respondents indicated that they had some difficulty using the system and that the support given within the game could be improved. Users that had difficulty however stated that in their second and third attempts at levels they felt more confident in using the systems and following the outlined tasks.

The feedback regarding confidence was encouraging, however the feedback of the systems positive impact to not align with the confidence results. This however was expected due to the nature of the question, while many users feel they benefitted from using the system, it also highlighted some areas in which users could be presenting themselves as potential targets for phishing attacks. When becoming aware of this some users felt less confident within phishing attacks and general security. This result however can be seen as positive as "overconfidence" can cause users to be even more vulnerable to these types of attack.

When asked if the respondent felt more aware of phishing attacks and general security most respondents (77.77%) selected yes from the feedback options. When asked to provide additional feedback, a large majority of the users that selected "No" to this option explained that they were already aware of many of these security issues. Many of these users considered themselves "technical" and also had prior knowledge of security and phishing issues.

User feedback regarding level difficulty is also encouraging, however it is clear that more "balancing" could be performed. The majority of users (44.44%) stated that the game was of an "average" difficulty, 22.22% that it was easy and 11.11% that the game was difficult. Within the extreme boundaries 11.11% of users state the game was very easy and 5.55% that it was very difficult. This range of figures is expected due to testing being performed on a "mixed" ability group with different levels of prior awareness. In future implementations further testing can be performed in an attempt to move more users from boundary values, to give a more suitable difficulty level.

Using the feedback provided by users, an average score was calculated for the first, second and third score (each attempt). The results show a clear increase with each play-through of the game, while this does not directly equate to "increased awareness" it does show that users are more able to use the system to educate themselves each time. User feedback also shows that users did not often fail within the same areas on their second and third attempts. This was particularly clear within URL levels, many users approached these levels with little to no experience of how to identify phishing URLS. While many users failed within these areas on their first attempts, they were unlikely to do so on second and third attempts. This was not only on the same level itself but also on the "type" of level, for instance if a user failed on a URL drag and drop level, they were less likely to fail on a URL question level.

5.2   Conclusions from User Testing

Overall these results support both the concept of interactive systems as educational tools, while also verifying that the system itself can be effective. While it would not be possible to measure the direct impact that the system could have without further research, users suggest that they would be more careful in approaching phishing attacks and more aware in general of how to spot them.

6   Conclusion and Future Work

In conclusion the project can be seen as a success, not only did the system meet the desired requirements, but also according to user feedback, the individuals both enjoyed and benefitted from using the system.

While effective testing was also performed on users before and after using the system, this test process could be improved. One way to do so would be to increase the user group from 18 to a more substantial figure, this could be possible as a future development to more accurately access the system. Another way the process could be improved would be through more accurate and specific questioning regarding current user experience and their experience of the system. While the current questionnaire format yielded strong results, more accurate and specific questions could access areas in which the system could be improved.

Further research that could be applied using this type of interactive system could be to evaluate the effectiveness of interactive systems within the context of phishing, social engineering and general security. While this was not possible within the timescale of the current project, this is a future development that would not only measure its effectiveness as a solution, but also the effectiveness of interactive systems in general.

7   References

Anandpara, K., Dingman, A., Jakobsson, M., Liu, D. & Roinestad, H., (2007). *Phishing IQ tests measure fear, not ability*. Berlin : Springer Berlin Heidelberg. p362-366.

CSO, 2011. *The Ultimate Guide to Social Engineering*. [pdf] Available at: < http://bit.ly/LRRgkN> [Accessed 20 January 2013].

Gorling, S. 2006. *The myth of user education*. In Proceedings of the 16th Virus Bulletin International Conference

Hadnagy, C., 2011. *The Art of Human Hacking*. [pdf] Available at: < http://bit.ly/15wBOG8 > [Accessed 25 January 2013].

Kumaraguru, P. Cranshaw, J., Acquisti, A., Cranor, L., Hong, J., Blair, M. A., and Pham, T., 2009. *School of Phish: A Real-World Evaluation of Anti-Phishing Training*. In the Proceedings On Usable Privacy and Security.

Milletary, J., 2005. *Technical Trends in Phishing Attacks*. [pdf] Available at: < http://bit.ly/15yipK1 > [Accessed 22 January 2013].

Plohmann, D., Leder, F. & Gerhards-Padilla, E., 2011. *Botnets: Detection, Measurement, Disinfection & Defence*. [pdf] Available at: <http://goo.gl/AFgCf2> [Accessed 22 January 2013].

Sheng, S. Magnien, B. Kumaraguru, p. Acquisti, A. Cranor, L. F., Hong, J. & Nunge, E. 2007. *Anti-Phishing Phil: The Design and Evaluation of a Game That Teaches People Not to Fall for Phish* [Online.] Available at: < http://bit.ly/eywVmL > [Accessed 22 January 2013].

Symantec, 2013. *Symantec Intelligence Report: January 2013*. [Online.] Available at: < http://bit.ly/15heiPp > [Accessed 22 January 2013].

Speech with Gesture of a Robot in HRI

Q.Renon and T.Belpaeme

School of Computing and Mathematics, Plymouth University, Plymouth, UK
e-mail: tony.belpaeme@plymouth.ac.uk

Abstract

The future of Robotics is to make robots socials. A social robot can interact with humans by using the same ways of communication. Gesture is one the way that humans use to communicate between each other. This project deals with the development of a tool that enable a user to make the humanoid robot Nao, from the French society Aldebaran Robotics, to gesture while speaking. This project has also realized a product test about the developed tool to get the feelings of peoples in front of a gesturing robot. In this project we are considering the hypothesis that people pay attention to the synchronisation between gestures and the speech of a humanoid robot.

Keywords

HRI, Robotics, Nao, Gestures, Speech

1   Introduction

Robots are more and more used in our private and working environment and we often have to use them. However we do not really interact with them. Providing the same ways of communication than human's can help robots to interact with us and reciprocally. Currently, the humanoid robot Nao from the French society Aldebaran Robotics is one of the must used robot by Universities and researchers. They use this robot to make some research in lots of domains as Robotics and Psychology. This robot is really powerful and easy to use by the researchers. However, it is currently unable to realize a gesture that matches with the content of its speech.

This project aims to create a tool that enables a user to easily make the Nao gesture while speaking.

2   Humans' spontaneous gestures

To be able to make a robot gesture as humans, we need to understand how humans gesture. We can find four main types of gestures that humans do during a speech. These kinds of gestures are named "Iconic gesture", "Metaphoric gesture", "Beat gesture" and "Deictic gesture". The Iconic gesture represents the meaning of an action that is described by the speaker. In the case where a speaker talks about a specific action, he will naturally mimic the action he is currently describing. A speaker use metaphoric gestures to make the listener imagine the situation which he his describing. As example, he can use his hands to draw in the air the different objects described in its speech. The beat gestures are the little movements that we all do while speaking. These gesture do not depend with the content of the speech but only deals with the rhythm of the speech. The deictic gesture is the last kind of gestures that humans do. This kind of gesture is the one we use to point an object or a direction in our environment.

3   Design of social robots

To be social, robots need some tools to interact with humans. However, all their bodies can affect the interactions. Social robots need to have an embodiment and a specific anthropomorphism (Feil-Seifer & Matari´c, 2009). As social robots aims to interfere in humans' environment, it seems more practical they look like humans. However, humans feel more and more sympathy to a robot until a certain point of likeliness. This effect is described by the following graph named the "Uncanny valley".

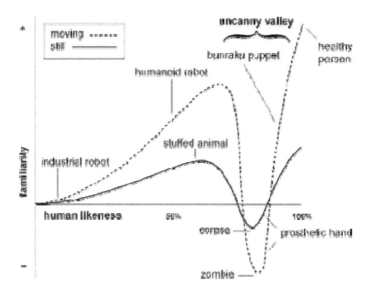

Figure 1: The uncanny valley (Masahiro Mori, 1970)

4   Programming a Nao robot

The Nao is a humanoid robot created by the French society Aldebaran Robotics. It is programmable with many languages that are Urbi, C++, Java, Python, MATLAB and .Net. Programming the Nao consists in using the different objects implemented on the Nao or to directly set the values of its motors. Theses objects are named UObject and works as servers the programs can access. In this project, we decided to program the tool in Urbi and C++. The Nao can receive Urbi commands via its port 54000.

Here is a scheme of the Nao's joints and features:

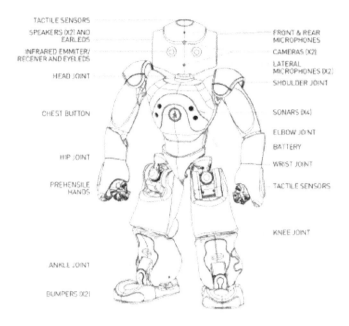

Figure 2: Nao's features (Aldebaran Robotics)

5 Specifications

The tool developed in this project is written in C++ and Urbi. It consists in providing some functions to a user to enable him to make the Nao robot gesture while speaking. The gesture can be chosen or automatically selected during the speech.

We decided to create 2 Urbi functions named 'ttswg' and 'auto_ttswg'. The user calls these functions by sending Urbi commands on the port 54000 of the Nao.

The tool makes also the Nao move a little bit, track faces and blinking when it does not speak.

The user functions works by using tagged words included either manually included in the text of the speech for the ttswg function or automatically for the auto_ttswg one.

6 Design

The tool is constituted of an Urbi file loaded on the Nao and a C++ UObject named 'multi_tag_extractor' that runs on a the personal computer the user uses to send Urbi commands to the Nao. Once loaded and run on the Nao, the 'u_ttswg.u' file makes the Nao do some background tasks and provide to the user the two functions 'ttswg' and 'auto_ttswg'. The multi_tag_extractor object is used by the ttswg function to detect and extract the tagged words contained in the text of the speech.

The background tasks make the Nao oscillate, do a face tracking and blinking.

6.1 Background tasks

The u_ttswg.u file makes, once loaded, the Nao do the background tasks. The oscillations of the whole body of the Nao use all its motors. Because of these oscillations, the system needs to manage the case where the motors are accessed by two different functions at the same time. To do this, we have decided to divide the body of the Nao in 5 parts: head, legs and arms. A global variable named 'mutex' is created in the Urbi file. This variable is a table of 5 boxes, one for each part of the robot and contains either '0' or '1'. When a box of this table is set to 0, the corresponding part of the Nao oscillates.

The oscillation background task consists in making the Nao move little movements while standing without speaking. The oscillations is simply a change of the motors' values by following sinusoidal functions that have a specific amplitude and period for each part of the Nao's body.

The face tracking makes the Nao follow the face of the nearest person in front of him. A UObject 'FaceTracker' already exists on the Nao and the u_ttswg.u file just use its functions.

The eye blinking is just a periodic switch of the Nao's eyes every 4 seconds.

6.2 The ttswg function

The ttswg function is a user function that takes as parameter a text provided by the user. This text can contain some tagged words that make the Nao gesture while speaking. The gesture that is defined by the tagged word is played at the same time than the text read by the Nao that is situated just before the tagged word. Consequently, the text given as parameter has to be composed with a series pair's text/tagged word. To be sure the user respect this format, the function automatically add a space print at the beginning of the text and also a space print followed by a tagged word at the end. The automatically added tagged word at the end of the text makes the Nao do not move. To work, the ttswg function use the function analyse_text of the multi_tag_extractor object that runs on the personal computer of the user. The analyse_text function split the text given in part that are placed into 2 tables named 'sentences' and 'tagged_words'.

Here is a sheme that shows the splitting realized by analyse_text function:

First sentence <First_tagged_word> second sentence <Second_tagged_word> <NOTHING>

sentences	First sentence	Second sentence	(space)		

Tagged_word	First_tagged_word	NOTHING			

Figure 3: Repartition of parts of a text between 'sentences' and 'tagged_words' tables

The ttswg function only make the Nao speak the text contained in the box of the table 'sentences' and play at the same time the gesture defined by the tagged word written in the same number of the box of the 'tagged_words' table.

6.3 The auto_ttswg function

The auto_ttswg function is a user function that allows the user to make the Nao gesture during a speech as the ttswg function does but without having to add tagged words into the text. In fact the auto_ttswg function use the autoTagging function from the multi_tag_extractor to automatically add tagged words into the text and then call the ttswg function to make the Nao speak and gesture with the new text provided by the autoTagging function.

The autoTagging function automatically adds some tagged words into the text in function of its content. The tagged words are place into the text after some known words for which there is matching gestures. Moreover, if there is not any known word into the text for a while, a tagged word, that make the Nao move a little bit, is added into the text. These little gestures can be interpreted as beat gesture because they do not have really meaning. These beat gesture are added every 4 words if there is not 'known word' before. Moreover, the autoTagging function do not add the tagged word after some linking words as 'the', 'for', 'a', 'an', 'to' and 'on'.

The user can of course give a text that contains some tagged words to the auto_ttswg function but it can make the Nao gesture twice the same gesture or two consecutive gestures if the tagged word manually added into the text is situated after a known word.

7 Product test

7.1 Specification and design

For this project, a product test was realized to get the feelings of people looking at the Nao gesturing thanks to the ttswg function. This product test is designed as a between subject experiment and uses 3 videos and a survey.

The first video is just a record of the Nao gesturing thanks to the ttswg function with a specific text that contains manually added tagged words. The two others videos are copies of the first one but with the sound shifted with the image. In the first case the sound is played 2 seconds before the image and in the second case the sound is delayed of 2 seconds. The product test works by providing an online survey to the testers. The testers were recruited thanks to social networks as Facebook and tweeter and also family and friends of friends. Also, we did not check the technical knowledge of the respondents. Familiarity with robots and technology or the lack thereof, might have an influence on their responses. This survey distributes a random video between the three videos and the user is not allowed to redo the survey. In reality, there are 3 videos in English and 3 in French. The meaning of the speech is essentially the same and the gestures used are exactly the same. The first question of the survey is the choice of the language for the videos and the questions. This survey also asks some general information about the tester as his age, gender and country. Here are the 6 criteria the tester has to evaluate about the videos he must watch:

- Q1: Quality of the speech

- Q2: How natural is the gesture of the robot while speaking?

- Q3: The correspondence between gestures and speech

- Q4: Friendliness of the robot

- Q5: How natural is the gesture of the robot when it is not speaking (at the beginning and the end of the video)?

- Q6: The synchronization between gestures and the speech

The tester gives marks between 1 and 10 for each criterion. To be sure the tester has watch the good video until its end, a number is displayed at the end of the video and the tester must enter this number in another question of the survey.

The gestures used in the video are iconic gestures and almost beat gestures. The gestures chosen in the video are provided by a library of gestures that does not contain other kind of gestures. We use gestures that make the Nao move a little bit its arms as if these ones were beat gesture. We also used some iconic gestures that make the Nao wave its hands to say hello and goodbye and make it bent to say "thank you".

7.2 Results

There are 57 people over 9 different countries and between 20 and 50 years old that have completed the survey. However most of them (45) are French people and the others who choose the English survey are only 12. Here is a table that show the average results for each question for the French survey:

	Q1	Q2	Q3	Q4	Q5	Q6
Fr-Video 1	6,69230	4,923076	5,6923076	8,53846	5,461538	6,153846154
Fr-Video 2	8,3125	5,5625	5,875	8,6875	5,875	4,625
Fr-Video 3	6,8125	5,5	4,5625	8,625	6,9375	4,6875
Total	7,31111 1	5,355555	5,3555555	8,62222	6,133333	5,088888889
Ranking	2,3,1	2,3,1	2,1,3	2,3,1	3,2,1	1,3,2

The results of the English survey are quite similar than the French results. There are only 3 questions where we can compare the different videos, the second, the third and the sixth. For the others, the answer should not depend on the videos because these questions take care of the speech or the gesture separately or are too global.

As the aim of the tool is to make the gesture played by the Nao match with the content of the speech, the most important questions are the third and the sixth ones. The best results about the synchronization are obtained by the application without any shift of the sound. However, it is interesting to notice that people consider the correspondence between the gesture and the speech is better when the sound is in advance compare with the image. The fact that people dissociate the correspondence and the synchronisation could be explained by the fact that the gestures played by the Nao are not meaningful enough. About the natural of the robot gesturing while speaking, French and English testers have different results. French testers consider the gesture of the robot while speaking more natural when the sound is in advance but English testers prefer the original video. About the other questions, English testers have better mark the quality of the speech of the robot in their videos than the Frenchs with their own. However, French testers consider the Nao friendlier than English people. About the background task that makes the Nao oscillating when it does not speak, have not very appreciate it. However, a colleague told us in the comment section of the survey that it looks much worse in the video than in real.

Moreover, we have realized a statistical analysis of the data and of the variance (ANOVA). To realize this analysis, as we did not have the same numbers of testers for each video, we removed the answers of three testers for each question for the video 2 and 3 to have 13 testers for each video and questions. To choose the answers we removed, we eliminated the furthest from the mean answers.

Finally thanks to this survey, we can say that the tool created during this project is a good way to synchronize gestures with a speech but it needs to have much more gestures and to improve the meaning of these gestures. The robot should also have all kind of gestures as beat and metaphoric gestures that can lake at the moment.

8 Conclusion

Thanks to this project we have provided to the ALIZ-E research team, a tool they could use to make some experiments or presentations of the Nao robot and to help understanding the aim of gesture in human-robot interactions.

The product test realized in this project allowed us to target the different points to improve. The results of this test showed that the gestures of the applications do not correspond enough with the speech of the robot. It could be also interesting to add some metaphoric gesture and true beat gesture. However the application seem to be quite efficient to synchronize the gesture with the speech.

The project is far to be finished but helped to understand the gestures in HRI.

About the tool that has been created during this project, there are many ways to improve it. It could be interesting in adding more all-made gestures and the list of known words that includes adding tagged words. Even the gestures could be improved. As human, we interrupt a gesture to begin another one and can create naturally gestures to mime a situation or represent an object. These kinds of gestures would be really efficient for a robot to interact with humans. Moreover, the speech of the robot could be more fluent. About the product test, it may be interesting to redo the survey with much more people with different cultures and by asking if people use to work in the domain.

9   References

Aldebaran Robotics, n.d. *Documentations*. [Online] Available at: http://www.aldebaran-robotics.com/en/Discover-NAO/datasheet.html [Accessed 06 June 2013].

Feil-Seifer, D. & Matari´c, M.J., 2009. Human-Robot Interaction. In Meyers, R.A. *Encyclopedia of Complexity and Systems Science*. New york: Springer. pp.4643-59.

Mori, M., 1970. The Uncanny Valley. *Energy*, pp.33-35.

Beat Gestures with Sentiment

G.Winser and T.Belpaeme

School of Computing and Mathematics, Plymouth University, Plymouth, UK
e-mail: tony.belpaeme@plymouth.ac.uk

Abstract

This aims of this research project were to look into beat gestures, how they are used in speech and if they could convey a change in sentiment. This is to provide research for the development of gestures used in conversational agents. A lot of research has been performed in different types of gesture but not in beat gestures. Previous research indicated that, although beat gestures traditionally only keep rhythm in conversation, they are used for providing emphasis on important and key points. I study was set up to see if there was a change in the perceived sentiment of a spoken phrase with differences in the size of beat gestures. This provided a significant result, that suggested that a chopping beat gesture cause a shift in perception towards anger or negative sentiment. Using the findings of the research, a study was undertaken into how sentiment may be detected for a given phrase to say and how to apply that sentiment to gesture to make sure it is conveyed to the conversational partner.

Keywords

Analysis, C++, Beat, Gestures, Java, Nao, Sentiment, Urbi

1   Introduction

Is communication just the speaking and listening of words? Or is there more to it? Gesture is used to convey just as much information as the words being spoken, if not more. A simple gesture can turn the entire mood of a conversation upside down or imply different meanings, with no difference in the words being said, or the intonation. This is a field of robotics that needs to be studied if the field of human - robot interaction is to grow and gain a foothold for the future. The very act of gesturing while talking is as natural as eating, breathing and sleeping for humans. It has been around for as long as spoken language, if not even before! Therefore, research needs to be conducted to further and better the field of robotics and human robot interaction. it has long been known that gestures have been around for a long time. It is actually suggested that a spoken language system developed from a gesture based communication system (Corballis, 2002).

Gestures have long been known to accompany speech when communicating ideas. There are 4 types of gesture that exist: Iconic, Deictic, Metaphoric and Beat gestures (Carter & University, 2012). Iconic gestures are used to represent attributes, for instance, widening your arms while saying "it was very wide" is one example of an iconic gesture. Deictic gestures are used to connect speech to an idea, or object. An example of this would be to say "look over there" while pointing to a point of interest. Metaphoric gestures are used to turn an abstract idea into a more concrete, relatable form. One such example would be to make a heart symbol an place it upon ones chest while uttering the words "I love you". The last type of gesture, and the type that this study will be concentrating on is the Beat gesture. These are not used to convey information but rather used to dictate emphasis or rhythm of the speech.

This paper will concentrate on beat gestures, and whether they can be used to alter the perception of sentiment with spoken phrases. Beat Gestures have long been known to dictate the rhythm of the conversation, but they have also been shown that to be used in direction giving to emphasise important points in the route being described to the listener (Brandhorst & Theune, 2009). This shows that although a beat gesture does not convey information, it can add valuable semantic meaning to a conversational exchange, in the form of emphasis or importance. There is also research to support the case that gesturing is almost exclusively in the realm of speaking, and that gesturing very infrequently happens during a conversational agents listening phase (McNeill, 1992). This implies that the gesturing process is very strongly linked with the conveying of information or meaning, and not in the ability to comprehend.

This paper will explore the question "Does a change in beat gesture affect the perceived sentiment of a spoken phrase". The hypothesis is that it will cause a significant difference.

2 Methodology

The experiment is to investigate whether the change in gesture will affect the perceived sentiment of the sentence that has been said. The experiment will capture the required data needed to assess the hypothesis. In respect to this individual experiment there are many factors to consider, such as:

- What sentence will be said

- What Gesture will be performed

- What timing will the gesture have

- What is the emphasis of the gesture.

These are just some of the factors that have to be considered. To be able to call the experiment fair, the same scenario should be presented but with one thing changing. This is going to be the sentence that is being said and the amplitude of the movement.

2.1 Hardware

The hardware that will be utilised is the Nao Robot from Aldebaran Robotics (Robotics, 2013). The Nao is a fully capable robotic platform that is ideal for research, as it has a powerful operating that runs URBI and is capable of easily executing speech and movement at the same time.

2.2 Software

The software that was developed was using the Java API for the NaoQi framework that Aldebaran have developed for the Nao. The software was written in java to give the power of external processing, but interfacing with the Urbi Server on the robot. This is because Urbi is incredibly powerful and once a command is sent, it is run server side. This methodology for performing the computation on the external computer, creating a command and sending it to the Urbi server means that a full program can be sent to the robot and a minimum of delay occurs while processing. Otherwise if it was all run from the external machine, there would be noticeable delays.

2.3 Experiment Conditions

In the experiment, the only things that are changing are the speech and the amplitude of the gesture that is being performed. For the purposes of the experiment, the difference in the gesture movement must be very noticeable. Because of this, the gesture movements shall be taken from both ends of the scale, with maximum and minimum movement amounts represented. This is to make the experiment as diverse as possible. The two sentences that will be said are listed in the table below, they will be accompanied by large and small movements, and then these results will be compared. The movements start off with the arm just below horizontal, and then moving downwards and back up to the starting position again.

As there are 2 variables within the experiment, each with two distinct values, that means that there are 4 conditions required to cover every possibility. If you include the 2 control conditions, this creates the following conditions.

Spoken Sentence	Beat Gestures Performed
"You must do your exercises tomorrow."	None
"You will do better next week"	None
"You must do your exercises tomorrow."	Small
"You will do better next week"	Small
"You must do your exercises tomorrow."	Large
"You will do better next week"	Large

Table 1: Experimental Conditions

This provides all the needed combinations to be able to collect data and perform a complete analysis.

The conditions are presented to the participants in the form of a video, the videos are designed to be as plain as possible, with the robot looking at the camera. This is to direct attention to the robot on the screen and focus the participant. The experimental video setup is as follows:

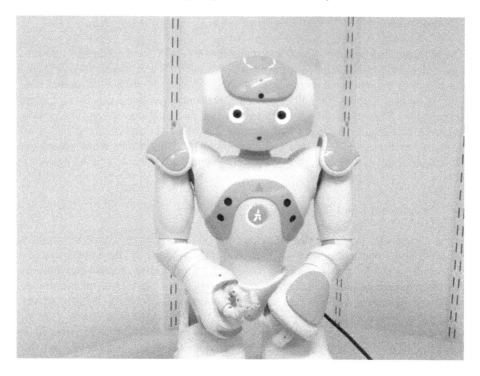

Figure 1: Experimental video setup

With each video, the participants are asked the following questions.:

- Is the robot: Angry - Calm.

- Is the robot: Discouraging - Encouraging

- Is the Robot: Telling you off - Being Kind?

- Is its behaviour: Unnatural - Natural

- Is the robot being: Positive - Negative

Each answer option was at opposite ends of a 5 point scalar response.

These questions were formed into an online survey. The survey was run as a repeated measures test, where each participant answered questions about every condition. The conditions were randomised however to try and eliminate any leading effect.

The Survey was advertised on Facebook, and also on Reddit, which is an online bulletin site with a global audience. This means that the responses will be from people that are not necessarily in the field so will give impartial, unbiased responses.

The survey was run for 5 days, during which, 65 responses were collected. After inspection however, it appeared that 9 of those responses were incomplete. These incomplete responses were culled from the data to preserve data integrity and to only deal with complete responses to make it easier for the statistical analysis.

Although 5 questions are asked, only the questions regarding how angry or calm the robot it and how positive or negative it is being is of interest. These are the two main questions which will be used for statistical analysis.

3   Results & Analysis

The results immediately showed that when movement was concerned, the robot was perceived as more negative and angry in the conditions that had movement and speech.

The data for all the control conditions was similar, with all the responses lying with the median point of the scale, if ever so slightly on the negative side of the scale.

What was noticeable was that in the two questions of interest, which related to perceived emotion and sentiment respectively, the mean values were skewed more towards the negative end of the scale than the control tests. The other 3 questions data were fairly

The Data overall is fairly consistent, and does not appear to show much variation in the responses between the conditions. Two questions look interesting to explore further, The first question " Is the robot : Angry: Calm?" and also the question stated before, "Is the robots behaviour: Positive: Negative". These are suitable to be investigated as they showed a good amount of variance and also, could be linked, as emotion can be linked to sentiment (Thelwall & Buckley, 2010).

To see if the results were statistically significant, they were run through a 1 way ANOVA function, The positivity - negativity question returned a p value of:

$$p = 0.0083 < 0.05$$

and the question about how angry or calm the robot was returned a p value of :

$$p = 1.59151 * 10^{-7} < 0.05$$

These are both below the threshold of 0.05 so they contain some statistically significant results. To find out which conditions were statistically significant, they output from the ANOVA function was passed through a post hoc Tukey test. These returned the following charts:

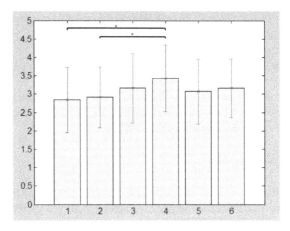

Figure 2: Positivity Post Hoc Tukey Test

The above graph shows that the responses for condition 4 ("You will do better next week" with large gestures), and the question "Is the robots Behaviour: Positive : Negative" which are the are significantly more negative than the responses for the same question for the control conditions. No other conditions were found to be statistically significant. The hypothesis looks plausible, but cannot be confirmed as it would be assumed that if a solid link between sentiment and beat gestures, then condition 6 would be significantly different than its control, which is condition 2.

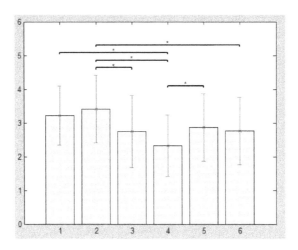

Figure 3: Post Hoc Tukey Test on Emotion Data

As seen in Figure 3, there is a large amount of significance. If you trace the lines from condition 2, every condition with movement is significantly different to it. This shows that the movement causes a big shift in the perception of the emotion of the robot. The robot pauses slightly between the end of the beat gesture and speech segment before starting the new beat gesture and speech sentence in the video for a condition that includes movements. This is not a product of design, but of the performance of the system as it ends one programming block and begins another.

Timing has been shown to be very important in the perception and comprehension of gesture, so maybe this involuntary pause has some effect on the perceived emotion. This introduces a confound into the experiment, which could affect the results. This could be eliminated in future iterations by copying the audio from a condition with movement onto the video for the control conditions, thus ensuring that they are completely identical. From the figure above, it can be seen that the larger movements do cause the perceived emotion to be more towards angry than calm

4 Conclusion

Although the research did show that in the perceived positivity or negativity of the robot between the first control condition and the condition with the same sentence with large beat gestures, it was expected that the significance would be mirrored between the second control and condition 6. This however, was not the case. Therefore the research suggests that the movement does affect the perceived sentiment of the sentence, but cannot confirm it. The non significance with the second control may be that the type of phrase may not have been appropriate for the research or may simply not be affected as much by movement as the phrase used in the first control condition. Further research is suggested into different types of phrases and how they are affected by movement, to gain a full understanding of this issue and how it may be controlled. It was found however that even though there was not a huge amount of significance, the moment movement was entered into the equation, the mean values of the perceived positivity and negativity all became skewed towards negative.

The area of emotion was explored also, as emotion can be linked to sentiment, and are often interchanged with one another in casual reference. There was found to be lot of statistical significance between the control conditions and the test cases that had movement within them, with every condition with movement being significant of control condition 2. The conditions with movement were significantly perceived as more angry than the control conditions, with the conditions with large movement perceived as being angrier than the test conditions that had small movements in. Suggestions for further research are to research if timing between movement and speech stages, between when a gesture and speech stop, and begins the next speech and gesture combination, affects the perception of emotion or sentiment. The research therefore:

- Suggests, but does not confirm that beat gestured performed with speech, do affect the perceived positivity or negativity of the statement, although further research is needed to confirm.

- That beat gestures, when combined with spoken phrases, are found to change the perceived emotion of the agents behaviour significantly towards the negative end of the scale, in this case anger over calmness.

- Bigger Gestures appear to cause the perceived sentiment and emotion to be more negative. Therefore it is suggested that if an autonomous system were to be designed, then large gestures should be linked towards negative sentiment phrases.

5 References

Brandhorst, C., & Theune, M. (2009). Beat Gestures in Direction Giving. *The 8th international gesture ...*, 1–8.

Carter, R., & University, C. (2012). Types of Gesture. Retrieved August 26, 2013, from https://sites.google.com/a/students.colgate.edu/gesture-brain-and-language/home/types-of-gestures

Corballis, M. (2002). *From hand to mouth: The origins of language*.

McNeill, D. (1992). *Hand and mind: What gestures reveal about thought*.

Robotics, A. (2013). Aldebaran Robotics. Retrieved August 24, 2013, from http://www.aldebaran-robotics.com

Thelwall, M., & Buckley, K. (2010). Sentiment strength detection in short informal text. *Journal Of The American Society For Information Science And Technology*, *61*(12), 2544–2558. doi:10.1002/asi

TCP Implementations Evaluation and Optimisation

T.Yu and B.V.Ghita

Center for Security, Communications and Network Research,
Plymouth University, Plymouth, United Kingdom
e-mail: info@cscan.org

Abstract

As a reliable transmission protocol, Transmission Control Protocol (TCP) is widely used in the Internet today. Variety of TCP implementations were developed to give better performance with the continuously increasing of traffic volume of Internet. In this project, eight TCP implementations are tested on the Network Simulator 2 platform, which include TCP-Tahoe, TCP-Reno, TCP-New Reno, TCP-Vegas, TCP-Linux, TCP-Sack, TCP-Fack and TCP-Asym. Both of these TCP implementations uses different congestion control mechanism to deal with different types of performance issue while none of them can work outstanding under every type of network condition. Finally, their features of performance are briefly discussed.

Keywords

TCP, TCP agent, TCP implementation, Throughput, Queue-limit, Congestion Control Algorithm, NS-2, Tcl, AWK.

1   Introduction

TCP is a connection-oriented reliable transport protocol which is widely used in the field of network, whatever for home or commercial applications. In order to prevent data congestion, the standard TCP protocol uses the collision detection technique to improve communication performance as much as possible. It is noteworthy that the development of the network environment presents the trend of diversification (e.g. LAN, xDSL, Cable, 3G Wireless and Optical Fibre) and the characteristics of each network environment is quite different from other network environments. That lead to the standard TCP congestion detection technique could not adapt to those network environments efficiently. So, a variety of different TCP implementations (they would be also called 'TCP agents') with the modified congestion detection mechanisms have been introduced to deal with this problem (e.g. TCP-Reno, TCP-New Reno, TCP-Tahoe and TCP-Vegas). These TCP implementations (also called TCP clients or TCP agents) were integrated by different operating systems (e.g. Ubuntu, Android, and Windows) due to the considerations of different groups of user and fields of application.

TCP is used by most of application protocols that require reliable transmission of all data, such as HTTP, FTP, SMTP and IMAP. Firstly, a TCP connection is built up after a success three-way handshake; then the packets are transmitted through the established virtual circuits. After data transmission is completed, this TCP connection will be terminated after a four-way handshake (Stewart & Metz, 2001) and all of the allocated resources will be released.

Congestion collapse is the typical problem with the TCP/IP networking environment, and it was initially identified in RFC No.896 document (Nagle, 1984). It also happens at the bottleneck points in the network, where the volume of the incoming traffic exceeds the processing performance of the networking device or the outgoing bandwidth. To deal with this type of problem from occurring, TCP uses mainly four congestion control algorithms, which are slow start, congestion avoidance, fast retransmit and fast recovery. **TCP Tahoe** was firstly proposed by Jacobson (1988). According to the theory from Jacobson, Tahoe would restart from the 'slow start' stage after the packet loss occurs to prevent the network from being overwhelmed by the burst traffic flows initially then the TCP connection would never get start. There are several problems of Tahoe's algorithm. Firstly, it uses much more time to detect and recognise the packet loss event. Secondly, the 'slow start' stage would increase the end-to-end delay and reduce the levels of link utilisation. **TCP Reno** was defined in the RFC No.2001 document, and it is slightly different from the standard TCP congestion control algorithm. The 'fast recovery' stage is once used an event of packet loss is found by the sending client that the Reno sending client will halve the value of 'cwnd' (but not to set the value of 'cwnd' to one max segment size, which would be implemented by a TCP Tahoe sending client), set the ssthresh equal to the value of 'cwnd', implement the fast retransmit and then enter the 'fast recovery' stage. Reno would have a performance downgrade when there are multiple packet loss events happen in the same window as the Reno sending client will only retransmits one single packet even there are multiple lost packet. **TCP New Reno** improves the performance of the 'fast retransmit' stage and the 'fast recovery' stage in many types of network scenarios, especially in some situations of which the TCP clients are unable to support selective acknowledgement technology. The **TCP Vegas** implementation was defined on an IEEE journal by Brakmo and Peterson (1995). It is an implementation focusing on issues related to the end-to-end delays rather than the packet losses. The main differences between Vegas and Reno is that the Reno can only detects the network congestions by recognizing the packet losses which were already happened while the Vegas is able to judge that the congestion would happen soon. The main disadvantage of TCP Vegas is the reduction of the traffic throughput compared to the other TCP implementation caused by the mechanism of packet loss prediction. According to the related paper of introducing the **TCP Linux** (Wei & Cao, 2006), this type of TCP implementation enables the client to transmit the data much faster, and its processing behaviour is similar to the real Linux operating system as the source codes of the TCP congestion control algorithm of Linux kernels were embedded into the TCP Linux implementation. It has the standard interface to be more extensible and flexible than other implementation. It involved the new scoreboard called 'Scoreboard1' which combined the features of 'Scoreboard-RQ' and the Linux selective acknowledgement processing routine mechanism and it can detect the packet loss event more accurately than other implementations under a considerable packet loss rate of the network. The **TCP Sack** (Jacobson & Braden, 1988) is an attempt of implementing the selective acknowledgment strategy in TCP transmission. It integrates the selective acknowledgment method and the selective repeat retransmission method to solve the issue of losing the acknowledgment based timer after multiple segment losses. There are two new TCP options used by the TCP Sack implementation, which are the enabling option called 'SACK-Permitted' and the SACK option. **TCP Fack** (Andreasson, 2002) is an attempt to enable the 'Forward Acknowledgement' feature in Linux platform, and implementation in NS-2 enables researchers to simulate the client's performance with it efficiently without building a real Linux environment. Based on the working mechanism of standard TCP transmission, the issue of relying on ACKs for reliability and for congestion control was recognised to be the main problem of performance deduction over asymmetric networks (e.g. sometimes the ACKs don't come back fast enough or get lost). **TCP Asym** was worked out to focus on dealing with this type of issue.

The following chapter will introduce the design of testbed and experiments. Chapter 3 and chapter 4 will present the analysis of simulation results and additional case studies, followed by section 5 which draws conclusions and future work. It will be the noteworthy point of this paper that a fixed matrix of suggested TCP implementations will be provided at the end of chapter 4 which is generated based on the results of simulations and those additional case studies.

2   Testbed

All of the simulations are based on the Network Simulator 2 (NS-2) platform which was written in C++ and Otcl programming language. It will be used to run the generated simulation scenarios Since this project aims to investigate the performance of TCP implementations under the network situations of different packet loss rates, the experiments should establish the TCP connections under different settings of 'queue-limit' and delays. Thus the testbed is designed as shown as following figures. Firstly, TCP lab 2.1 and 2.2 are used to simulate the performance of TCP implementations under a short-distance backbone link individually and comprehensively with comprehensive background traffic while TCP lab 3.1 and 3.2 are used to simulate the performance of TCP implementations under a long-distance backbone link with multi-segment background traffic individually and comprehensively. As the combination tests, the topology of TCP lab 1.2 are shown in Figure 4

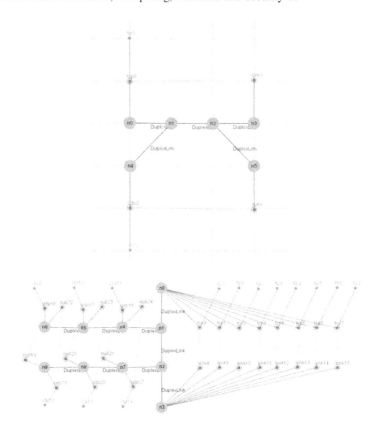

Figure 1: Topology of scenario – TCP lab 2.1 and lab 2.2

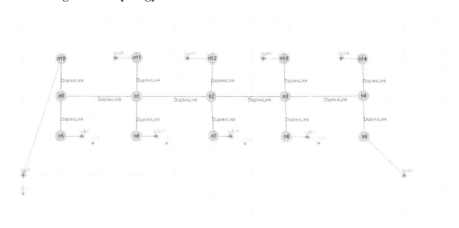

Figure 2: Topology of scenario – TCP lab 3.1

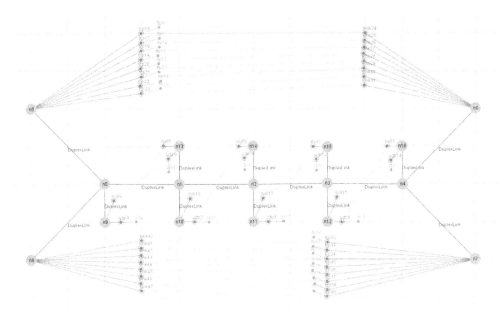

Figure 3: Topology of scenario – TCP lab 3.2

Detailed settings of these scenarios can be found as below.

(1) TCP lab 2.1 – Individual TCP Implementation
Core Link (between n1 and n2): Bandwidth 10Mbps, Delay 100 ms, Queue Limit 10, 20, 30, 40, 50.
Access Link (all other links): Bandwidth 100Mbps, Delay 50 ms
Length of Simulation: 30 seconds

(2) TCP lab 2.2 – Eight TCP Implementations
Core Link (between n1 and n2): Bandwidth 10Mbps, Delay 100 ms, Queue Limit 15, 30, 45, 60, 90
Access Link (all other links): Bandwidth 100Mbps, Delay 50 ms
Length of Simulation: 30 seconds

(3) TCP lab 3.1 – Individual TCP Implementation
Core Link (between n0 and n4): Bandwidth 15Mbps, Delay 400 ms, Queue Limit 10, 20, 30, 40, 50.
Access Link (all other links): Bandwidth 100Mbps, Delay 25 ms
Length of Simulation: 30 seconds

(4) TCP lab 3.2 – Eight TCP Implementations and Dual Directions
Core Link (between n0 and n4): Bandwidth 15Mbps, Delay 400 ms, Queue Limit 10, 20, 30, 40, 50.
Access Link (all other links): Bandwidth 100Mbps, Delay 25 ms
Length of Simulation: 30 seconds

3   Results Analysis

3.1   TCP lab 2.1#

TCP 2.1					
TCP Agent	QL=10	QL=20	QL=30	QL=40	QL=50
Tahoe(Kbps)	108.326	248.923	503.025	502.477	538.184
Reno(Kbps)	110.804	395.659	476.479	472.788	538.184
Newreno(Kbps)	182.5	430.325	510.833	510.285	538.184
Vegas(Kbps)	173.29	328.265	485.709	490.895	505.39
Linux(Kbps)	79.7895	213.913	1309.51	1286.02	1774.66
Sack1(Kbps)	171.539	485.672	514.179	513.631	538.184
Fack(Kbps)	67.617	179.289	485.547	483.931	538.184
Asym(Kbps)	110.657	430.282	516.688	513.611	538.184

Table 1: Average Throughput (TCP lab 2.1)

According to the Table 1, which represents the throughput results of eight TCP implementations under of five sub-scenario of the scenarios 1#. Based on the previous analysis of 'cwnd' performance, the corresponding result of throughput of sub-scenario 'QL=10' shows the Newreno client achieved the highest throughput, which was 182Kbps while the throughput of other seven TCP implementations were lower than this one. Also, the Vegas' 'cwnd' never be reset to '1' and kept calculating the network condition and maintain the throughput at a considerable level. It can be assumed that Vegas may be able to give the best user experience to users who have to use the transmission client under very limited networking resources and this hypothesis will be verified via the next three main scenarios (Scenario 2#, 3# and 4#).The competition became different from the second sub-scenario that the Newreno and Vegas clients were beyond by the Sack1 and Asym clients while the other clients were also reduced the gaps between their throughput performances and the winners' of previous sub-scenario. From the third sub-scenario, the results were entirely different from the previous two that the Linux client got the big-bang increasing and achieved the much higher throughput values of 1309.51 Kbps, 1286.02 Kbps and 1774.66 Kbps respectively while the other TCP clients only achieved the throughput volume under 540 Kbps. In contrast, Vegas client did not shows the apparent increasing while the 'queue limit' became higher and higher.

3.2   TCP lab 2.2#

TCP 2.2								
TCP Agent (Kbps)	Tahoe	Reno	Newreno	Vegas	Linux	Sack1	Fack	Asym
QL=15	202.355	231.4	246.145	161.104	218.37	244.444	188.547	**334.619**
QL=30	**472.492**	378.955	356.015	288.001	244.481	256.458	335.304	454.841
QL=45	287.002	372.825	338.016	314.84	**602.014**	409.193	338.496	364.541
QL=60	358.131	414.45	420.926	231.783	**644.978**	438.237	323.009	436.778
QL=90	463.324	530.347	441.919	341.715	**618.67**	455.547	345.472	396.523

Table 2: Average Throughput (TCP lab 2.2)

Based on the initial result of Table 1 in TCP lab 2.1, the following hypothesis might be worked out. TCP-Tahoe would have a mid-level performance under a network with little network resource and the jitter of the throughput will be extraordinarily high. Its performance would be increased significantly with the steady growth of network resources (e.g. queue limit) if there are only Tahoe clients in the network while the space of increasing of Tahoe may be squeezed by other implementations with the steady growth of network resources (e.g. TCP-Linux implementation).TCP-Reno and TCP-New Reno implementations are rather similar and achieved the similar marks. However, the jitter of throughput of these two implementations are better than TCP-Tahoe and TCP-Linux with little network resource, but they are worse than the Vegas even though the average throughput of Vegas are much lower than theirs under different levels of 'queue limit'. TCP-Vegas has no superiority or light spot on the peak value of 'cwnd', the average throughput or the predatory to the network resources. The most noteworthy point of it is that TCP Vegas has the best stability of throughput which can be found through the figures of 'cwnd' result. TCP-Linux is the best one which shows the noteworthy predatory to the network resources. This is not a feature which can be found when the network resource is not enough while the increasing of throughput and squeeze to other implementations will be seen as soon as the network resource become rich.

3.3   TCP 3.1 and 3.2

TCP 3.1					
TCP Agent	QL=10	QL=20	QL=30	QL=40	QL=50
Tahoe(Kbps)	34.4756	**91.4632**	**130.391**	134.572	169.955
Reno(Kbps)	46.4199	55.8881	102.529	109.029	169.955
Newreno(Kbps)	42.1542	81.4337	107.586	117.385	169.955
Vegas(Kbps)	**59.5675**	87.6715	61.1027	**144.796**	151.12
Linux(Kbps)	35.8542	73.2519	**143.665**	**144.569**	**294.221**
Sack1(Kbps)	44.0979	**110.122**	**144.873**	128.13	169.955
Fack(Kbps)	15.0845	56.3805	111.532	116.793	169.955
Asym(Kbps)	31.0199	**105.089**	111.213	148.216	169.955

Table 3: Average Throughput (TCP lab 3.1)

TCP 3.2 L2R								
TCP Agent (Kbps)	Tahoe	Reno	Newreno	Vegas	Linux	Sack1	Fack	Asym
QL=10	71.2125	**125.356**	36.4275	47.2497	86.0738	99.5477	99.706	44.9847
QL=20	**196.731**	137.23	96.0253	24.4	50.8308	108.637	129.89	74.9501
QL=30	**202.617**	*157.961*	73.6993	101.603	*189.491*	137.191	63.0903	84.4118
QL=40	**247.458**	*213.101*	120.713	50.4013	*188.583*	70.8569	60.5678	107.558
QL=50	**246.721**	*167.47*	127.341	96.0037	*185.428*	130.897	62.5468	125.418

Table 4: Average Throughput (TCP lab 3.2 - 1)

TCP 3.2 R2L								
TCP Agent (Kbps)	Tahoe	Reno	Newreno	Vegas	Linux	Sack1	Fack	Asym
QL=10	150.294	85.0664	203.47	77.7494	131.431	71.2608	59.1023	79.9423
QL=20	116.914	95.8922	248.822	113.112	124.132	73.9574	58.2602	51.7619
QL=30	97.4734	138.395	226.471	75.6624	134.016	60.4194	58.9282	84.5731
QL=40	98.5157	124.902	214.538	86.7713	129.102	69.1296	49.7076	101.302
QL=50	109.697	95.5068	247.665	42.5278	130.641	70.2502	48.8894	100.711

Table 5: Average Throughput (TCP lab 3.2 - 2)

Based on the results which were listed in the tables, the characteristics of these TCP implementations can be concluded as follows.

TCP-Tahoe would be able to keep its' client on a mid-range performance in terms of 'cwnd' and 'throughput' both in case of scarce network resources, or in the case of abundant network resources when there are not any other TCP implementations in the same route. But the key point is that, Tahoe would reset the value of 'cwnd' to the initial value as soon as the packet loss event being detected and this kind of self-adjustment activity can be found frequently. That means that the user experience (or availability) of some applications which are sensitive to the instantaneous throughput may be will be negatively affected from time to time. Tahoe's performance will be decreased to the low-end group when there are several different TCP implementations in the same route. However, there are some uncertainties for Tahoe's performance in the certain scenario (e.g. In the TCP Lab 3.2, Tahoe achieved different levels of performance in the sub-scenario L2R and R2L). There is a feature of Tahoe which can be noticed through the results that Tahoe could maintain a leading edge in case of scarce network resources. In most cases, the network resources more abundant, the speed of losing the leading-edge will be faster. So, it can be assumed that Tahoe is not suitable to be used for continuous data transmission (e.g. FTP downloading or Peer-to-Peer transmission).

TCP-Reno would be able to keep its' client on a higher mid-range performance in terms of 'cwnd' and 'throughput' compares to the performance of Tahoe in case of scarce network resources when there are not any other TCP implementations in the same route. In contrast, the Reno's performance would be decreased quickly with the increase of the network resources and it will be lower than Tahoe's. It can be found that Reno's performance will be still in the mid-range group when there are several different TCP implementations in the same route. However, the jitter of its congestion window is much lower than Tahoe's as 'fast recovery' stage is once used an event of packet loss is found by the sending client that the Reno sending client will halve the value of 'cwnd' rather than reset it to '1'. This enables Reno to be integrated into some operating systems which would be used to run the real-time applications as the jitter of throughput may be much better than Tahoe's.

TCP-New Reno is a similar implementation to TCP-Reno, and they may achieve the similar performance in most case. However, New Reno clients are traffic-environment sensitive ones, but they are not the queue-resource sensitive. TCP-New Reno does not have a strong ability to snatch network resources compared to TCP-Linux. There are no obvious weakness or advantages on New Reno's performance over these previous scenarios. The same as Reno, some real-time applications or mid-long term data transmission applications may perform well with these implementations.

TCP-Vegas achieved the totally different performance compared to any other TCP implementations which had been involved into this project. Vegas can keep its throughput on a stable level even in the case of poor network environment. The average throughput of Vegas is higher than other implementations under an extremely poor network condition, but it will soon become much lower than other implementations with the increase of the network resources. However, it can be assumed that TCP-Vegas is suitable for the implementation of low quality or medium quality real-time applications. For further research on the detailed results of simulations, as an example of this hypothesis, two totally different values of throughput of TCP-Vegas can be found in Table 1. TCP-Vegas achieved 173.29 Kbps of throughput when the 'queue-limit' was set to '10', and the result of it was higher than any other TCP implementations while it achieved 505.39 Kbps of throughput when the 'queue-limit' was set to '50' and the result of it was lower than any other TCP implementations. The fact can be used as an evidence that TCP-Vegas is not an aggressive TCP implementation which would occupy the network resources (e.g. bandwidth, transmission queues of routers) as much as possible.

TCP-Linux is an aggressive TCP implementation which would occupy the network resources (e.g. bandwidth, transmission queues of routers) as much as possible. But this predatory behaviour effectively embody specific data only if the network resource is not so poor. According to the previous tables, TCP-Linux was able to achieve the highest throughput from the third sub-scenario of each main scenario. For example, TCP achieved the significant higher throughput than any other implementations on 602 Kbps, 644 Kbps and 619 Kbps when the values of 'queue-limit' were set to '45', '60' and '90' respectively. There is a noteworthy point that TCP-Linux has the same weakness as TCP-Tahoe, which is TCP-Linux always reset the value of 'cwnd' to the initial value (it can be found that the value is '1' in this project as the curves shown in the figures) and the jitter of its throughput is significant high than Reno, New Reno and Vegas.

TCP-Sack is also an implementation suitable for using the real-time applications. Sack has similar throughput performance in common with TCP-Vegas when the network resources is exceptionally poor, and the value of throughput would be a little bit higher than Vegas'. But they are different in that, Sack demonstrated the strength of occupation of network resources while Vegas did not in the previous simulations. As a result of this, it can be assumed that Sack can fill in the demand for medium-quality and high-quality audio/video (real-time applications) communication or related applications which need the high throughput performance compared to Vegas'.

Based on the collected simulation results of previous tables, it can be summarised that TCP-Fack don't have the obvious leading place under all of the sub-scenarios regardless of whether the network resources is rich enough. Fack did not show a strong throughput performance if there are not any other TCP implementations in the same route, and it also achieved a lower result of throughput than other implementations when there are other TCP implementations in the same route as it seems that Fack was highly susceptible to the influence of other implementations. In addition, Fack would reset the value of 'cwnd' to '1' (the same activities as the Tahoe did) when the packet loss event happens.

TCP-Asym demonstrated the strength of occupation of network resources as TCP-Sack did in the previous simulations. In addition, Asym would reset the value of 'cwnd' to '1' (the same activities as the Tahoe and Fack did) when the packet loss event happens. As the results of this, Asym is suitable for using the high-volume data transmission applications while the medium-quality or high-quality real-time applications are not suitable to be used in an operating system which integrated Asym. As an exceptional choice, the low-quality real-time applications may choose the Asym as a backup one as its' feature of occupation of network resources may meet the requirements of short-length voice/video applications.

4   Additional Case Studies

4.1   Methodology

In real life, the data transmission activities which are based on TCP come across a variety of network environments. In order to discuss the actual performance of these TCP implementations in the actual network environments, the additional case studies will be implemented as below parts. However, several groups of specific parameters will be assigned to the links or routers of the scenarios so as to simulate the different types of actual networks (e.g. wireless/3G network, Ethernet LAN or Satellite network). The estimated values of round trip latency of Internet access would be calculated by checking the figures published by Brodkin (2013) and Rysavy (2005). However, the final result of the additional case studies and the results of previous individual simulations will be considered in order to work out the suggested TCP implementation matrix which will be listed in Table 6

Average RTT of Wired Network (e.g. fibre-to-the-home, cable-based, DSL-based) = (18 ms + 26 ms + 43 ms) / 3 = 29 ms (Typical bandwidth will be set to 10Mbps while the Packet loss rate will be set to 0.05%)

Average RTT of Satellite Network = (latest value of latency + older value of latency) / 2 = (638 ms + 1000 ms) / 2 = 1638 ms / 2 = 819 ms (Typical bandwidth will be set to 15Mbps, Packet loss rate will be set to 5%, 25%, 60%)

Average RTT of WCDMA (here the figures of WCDMA is used as the typical statistics of the widely used wireless network) = (200 ms + 300 ms) / 2 = 250 ms (Typical bandwidth will be set to 1.5Mbps while the Packet loss rate will be set to 0.05% and 0.5%)

4.2 Result of Case Studies

In the subjective test of wired network, Linux got the highest result in this wired network simulation and its performance is nearly doubled the performance of any other TCP implementations. This result can be used as an evidence to prove that the TCP-Linux is the best TCP implementation under the wired network access environment when the delay is exceptionally low (e.g. the delay in this case was set to 29 ms), and the bandwidth is the normal value of today's Ethernet/broadband network. TCP-Asym got the best result of the satellite test. It can be clearly seen that the performance of throughput were significant decreased with the increasing of the packet loss rate. However, the Vegas client got the similar performance of throughput when the values of packet loss rate were set to 5% and 25%, respectively. While Vegas got the winner place when the value of packet loss rate was set to 60%, which means the length between the sending device and the satellite was extremely long, and the connection was experiencing an unpleasant weather. Based on the results of throughput when the packet loss rate was set to 60%, it can be known that TCP-Linux and TCP-Fack did not perform well as the others' and the fact shows that the fault tolerances of these two TCP implementations are lower than the other six TCP implementations under the extremely high packet error/loss rate. Vegas took the first place again in this 3G/Wireless scenario with the results of highest throughput under two different degrees of packet loss rate. It can be inferred that Vegas has the better fault tolerance than the other seven TCP implementations, and it is suitable to be integrated into the operating system which would be installed on the mobile endpoint devices (e.g. Mobile phones, 3G/4G tablet PC, wireless routers/access points). At the same time, there were other five implementations achieved a considerable performance under these two values of packet loss rate, which were Asym, Sack1, New Reno, Reno and Tahoe. However, engineers may always attach the best one into the operating system, but these acceptable ones may be used under some special circumstances.

SUGGESTED TCP IMPLEMENTATIONS MATRIX

Packet Loss Rate	DELAY / BandW	0Kbps – 1Mbps	1Mbps – 2Mbps	2Mbps – 10Mbps	10Mbps – 100Mbps	100Mbps or Higher
PLR = 0% – 0.05%	<1ms – 125 ms	Vegas,Sack,Newreno	Vegas,Sack,Newreno,Asym	Sack,Newreno,Asym	Linux,Sack,Asym,Newreno	Linux,Sack,Asym,Newreno
	125 ms – 250 ms	Vegas,Sack,Newreno	Vegas,Sack,Newreno,Asym	Sack,Newreno,Asym	Linux,Sack,Asym,Newreno	Linux,Sack,Asym,Newreno
	250 ms – 1000 ms	Vegas,Sack,Newreno	Vegas,Sack,Newreno,Asym	Sack,Newreno,Asym	Linux,Sack,Asym,Newreno	Linux,Sack,Asym,Newreno
	1000 ms or higher	Vegas,Sack,Newreno	Vegas,Sack,Newreno,Asym	Sack,Newreno,Asym	Linux,Sack,Asym,Newreno	Linux,Sack,Asym,Newreno
PLR = 0.05% – 0.5%	<1ms – 125 ms	Vegas,Sack,Newreno,Asym	Vegas,Sack,Newreno,Asym	Sack,Newreno,Asym	Linux,Sack,Asym,Newreno	Linux,Sack,Asym,Newreno
	125 ms – 250 ms	Vegas,Sack,Newreno,Asym	Vegas,Sack,Newreno,Asym	Sack,Newreno,Asym	Sack,Asym	Sack,Asym
	250 ms – 1000 ms	Vegas,Sack,Newreno,Asym	Vegas,Sack,Newreno,Asym	Sack,Newreno,Asym	Sack,Asym	Sack,Asym
	1000 ms or higher	Sack,Asym,Vegas	Sack,Asym,Vegas	Sack,Asym,Vegas	Sack,Asym,Vegas	Sack,Asym,Vegas
PLR = 0.5% – 1%	<1ms – 125 ms	Sack,Asym,Vegas,Newreno	Sack,Asym,Vegas,Newreno	Sack,Asym,Vegas,Newreno	Linux,Sack,Asym,Newreno	Linux,Sack,Asym,Newreno
	125 ms – 250 ms	Sack,Asym,Vegas,Newreno	Sack,Asym,Vegas,Newreno	Sack,Asym,Vegas,Newreno	Linux,Sack,Asym,Newreno	Linux,Sack,Asym,Newreno
	250 ms – 1000 ms	Sack,Asym,Vegas	Sack,Asym,Vegas	Sack,Asym,Vegas	Sack,Asym,Vegas	Sack,Asym,Vegas
	1000 ms or higher	Sack,Asym,Vegas	Sack,Asym,Vegas	Sack,Asym,Vegas	Sack,Asym,Vegas	Sack,Asym,Vegas
PLR = 1% – 5%	<1ms – 125 ms	Sack,Asym,Vegas	Sack,Asym,Vegas	Sack,Asym,Vegas	Sack,Asym,Vegas	Sack,Asym,Vegas
	125 ms – 250 ms	Sack,Asym,Vegas	Sack,Asym,Vegas	Sack,Asym,Vegas	Sack,Asym,Vegas	Sack,Asym,Vegas
	250 ms – 1000 ms	Sack,Asym,Vegas	Sack,Asym,Vegas	Sack,Asym,Vegas	Sack,Asym,Vegas	Sack,Asym,Vegas
	1000 ms or higher	Sack,Asym,Vegas	Sack,Asym,Vegas	Sack,Asym,Vegas	Sack,Asym,Vegas	Sack,Asym,Vegas
PLR = 5% – 25%	<1ms – 125 ms	Sack,Asym,Vegas,Newreno	Sack,Asym,Vegas,Newreno	Sack,Asym,Vegas,Newreno	Sack,Asym,Vegas,Newreno	Sack,Asym,Vegas,Newreno
	125 ms – 250 ms	Sack,Asym,Vegas	Sack,Asym,Vegas	Sack,Asym,Vegas	Sack,Asym,Vegas	Sack,Asym,Vegas
	250 ms – 1000 ms	Vegas	Vegas	Vegas	Vegas	Vegas
	1000 ms or higher	Vegas	Vegas	Vegas	Vegas	Vegas
PLR = 25% or higher	<1ms – 125 ms	Vegas	Vegas	Vegas	Vegas	Vegas
	125 ms – 250 ms	Vegas	Vegas	Vegas	Vegas	Vegas
	250 ms – 1000 ms	Vegas	Vegas	Vegas	Vegas	Vegas
	1000 ms or higher	Vegas	Vegas	Vegas	Vegas	Vegas

Table 6: Suggested TCP implementations under different types of network conditions

5   Conclusions and future work

The background of TCP protocol and its congestion control mechanism was studied as a basic module of this project, and almost all of the other TCP implementations were developed based on the standard one. The difference between them is due to the different areas they targeted to (e.g. TCP-Vegas is mainly focus on increasing the transmission stability and dealing with the anti-Packet loss while TCP-Linux is mainly focus on snatching the network resources). Their actual performances under different network conditions were detailed studied in either individual scenarios or merged scenarios. From all of these studies, it can be concluded that there are not any one of these TCP implementations can work competent under all of the network conditions. So, the theoretical model of a TCP implementation management system was worked out and briefly described in order to develop a future direction of TCP performance optimisation. However, every TCP implementation has its own advantages and disadvantages. Thus, the researchers are still need to developing new implementations to meet the requirements of new networking types and featured applications with better algorithms to avoid the drawbacks.

6   References

Andreasson, O. (2002). Ipsysctl tutorial 1.0.4. Chapter 3.3.6. Available at: http://www.frozentux.net/ipsysctl-tutorial/chunkyhtml/tcpvariables.html [Date Accessed: 12/Aug/2013]

Brakmo, L. S., & Peterson, L. L. (1995). TCP Vegas: End to end congestion avoidance on a global Internet. Selected Areas in Communications, IEEE Journal on, 13(8), 1465-1480.

Brodkin, J. (2013). Satellite Internet faster than advertised, but latency still awful. Arstechnica.com. Available at: http://arstechnica.com/information-technology/2013/02/satellite-internet-faster-than-advertised-but-latency-still-awful/ [Date Accessed: 19/Aug/2013]

Jacobson, V. (1988, August). Congestion avoidance and control. In ACM SIGCOMM Computer Communication Review (Vol. 18, No. 4, pp. 314-329). ACM.

Jacobson, V., & Braden, R. T. (1988). TCP extensions for long-delay paths. ISI.

Nagle, J. (1984). RFC 896: Congestion control in IP. TCP internetworks (January 1984).

Rysavy, P. (2005). Data capabilities: GPRS to HSDPA and BEYOND. Whitepaper, Rysavy Research. Available at: http://www.rysavy.com/Articles/rysavy_data_sept2004.pdf [Date Accessed: 19/Aug/2013]

Stewart, R., & Metz, C. (2001). SCTP: new transport protocol for TCP/IP. Internet Computing, IEEE, 5(6), 64-69.

Stevens, W. R. (1997). TCP slow start, congestion avoidance, fast retransmit, and fast recovery algorithms. RFC2001. Available at: http://tools.ietf.org/html/rfc2001

Wei, D. X., & Cao, P. (2006, October). NS-2 TCP-Linux: an NS-2 TCP implementation with congestion control algorithms from Linux. In Proceeding from the 2006 workshop on ns-2: the IP network simulator (p. 9). ACM.

Author Index